"Jan Schnell's outstanding book is a grounded—   ...y into
the vocation of choreographing social change, assisted by the powers of
virtuous love and anger. It shares the fruit of extensive interviews, inviting
us into relationships with wise women who have devoted their lives as community organizers to protecting human dignity and strategically removing
causes of structural injustice. *Agapic Anger* is a discerning, captivating, and
transformational work."

—**Diana Fritz Cates**, professor of religion and ethics,
Department of Religious Studies, University of
Iowa, and author of *Aquinas on the Emotions*

"Since I was a girl, the messages I heard in my Latinx/Caribbean context
were 'don't complain,' 'don't get angry!' Anger and questioning aren't well
received if you're a woman. While other authors encourage the reader to
tame or control their anger, Jan Schnell's *Agapic Anger* gives people like me
permission to get outraged over injustice, without guilt or shame. Biblical
texts such as Proverbs 21:19 and 25:24 describe some women as 'contentious'
with no explanation of the cause. Such verses contribute to society's negative
perception of women. Schnell's proposal gives hope to women, redirecting
our anger toward community organizing for social transformation. *Agapic
Anger* is a must-read for women tired of being silenced by people afraid to
confront injustice."

—**Lydia Hernández-Marcial**, assistant professor
of Old Testament and Biblical Hebrew,
Seminario Evangélico de Puerto Rico

"Jan Schnell's timely argument in *Agapic Anger* is grounded in ethical and biblical
reflection, enriched by the practical wisdom of four women community organizers and written especially for those whose gendered experience can lure them to
'quail or quit' in the face of overwhelming obstacles. Schnell argues persuasively
that anger arising from the cry for a more just and loving world, disciplined by
specific practices of reflection and action and supported by community, can be
a healing and liberating force for personal and social transformation."

—**Kathleen D. "Kadi" Billman**, John H. Tietjen Professor of Pastoral
Ministry: Pastoral Theology, Emerita, Lutheran School of
Theology at Chicago, and coauthor of *Rachel's Cry:
Prayer of Lament and Rebirth of Hope*

"*Agapic Anger* weaves together stories, theology, ethics, scripture, and praxis to reframe how we view the power of anger in transforming communities and the world. Schnell challenges the gendered and racialized assumptions about anger, offering strategies for turning that passionate energy into a force for social change. Drawing on the experiences of women leading faith-based organizing, this book offers practiced wisdom on how to use love-rooted anger for the sake of the world."

—**Steve Jerbi**, OEF, director of the Organizing for Mission Network, and coordinator of community organizing, Evangelical Lutheran Church in America

"Drawing on the wisdom of women and gender-diverse people, *Agapic Anger* fosters a healthy relationship with both anger and those who are angry to bring about social transformation informed and shaped by the gospel of Christ. Artistic, persuasive, and reflective, *Agapic Anger* is a sincere pursuit to embrace anger as a moral emotion with a potential for positive and transformative change rooted in individual stories with a vision for collective impact."

—**Helen Chukka**, assistant professor of Hebrew Bible, Wartburg Theological Seminary

"Jan R. Schnell brings to life the voices of four dedicated women organizers, each story richly embodying their struggles, dreams, and unwavering commitment to their communities. For the faithful reader, the exposition on agapic anger reveals a powerful truth: that anger, when channeled properly within the confines of an organized community, becomes a catalyst for fostering transformative change caught up in the liberating love of Christ Jesus. The testimonies, philosophies, and cautions raised by Schnell provide wonderful guidance to communities organizing for the betterment of their neighborhoods."

—**Aaron Shoppa**, program director, Youth Ministry, Evangelical Lutheran Church in America

AGAPIC
ANGER

AGAPIC ANGER

Influencing Change While Navigating Gender

JAN R. SCHNELL

FORTRESS PRESS

MINNEAPOLIS

30   29   28   27   26   25   24   1   2   3   4   5   6   7   8   9

Library of Congress Cataloging-in-Publication Data

Names: Schnell, Jan Rippentrop, author.
Title: Agapic anger : influencing change while navigating gender / Jan R. Schnell.
Description: Minneapolis : Fortress Press, [2025] | Includes bibliographical references.
Identifiers: LCCN 2024029935 (print) | LCCN 2024029936 (ebook) |
   ISBN 9781506496702 (print) | ISBN 9781506496719 (ebook)
Subjects: LCSH: Anger--Religious aspects--Christianity. | Gender
   identity--Religious aspects--Christianity.
Classification: LCC BV4627.A5 S36 2025 (print) | LCC BV4627.A5 (ebook) |
   DDC 241/.6--dc23/eng/20241028
LC record available at https://lccn.loc.gov/2024029935
LC ebook record available at https://lccn.loc.gov/2024029936

Cover image: Compilation of stock illustrations from Getty Images
Cover design: Kristin Miller

Print ISBN: 978-1-5064-9670-2
eBook ISBN: 978-1-5064-9671-9

Contents

Part IV: Choreography of Agapic Anger

Prelude

A myelin sheath of ice coats the pericardium,
Frosty tendrils advancing unbidden,
Creeping beyond their coopted fortress
Draining the core's buoyancy.

Dread ice steals into limbs,
Pinning down,
Stopping the forward.

Sink.
Easiest to sink.

Down.
Cold.
Done.

But,
Buoyancy.
Its buoyancy.
This body's buoyancy.
A resilient fight lives in this chest.

The fight says, "No," and resistance is kindled.
The fight stands up, "NO," and it is warming.
The fight picks up, "You were wrong." A spark.
She remembers, "Your act is not my reduction."
She breathes. Oxygen ignites. "That was abuse."

Flicker, back in her eye,
Calls out the ice,
Cold tendrils,
Freezing lie that the shame of his act should drown her.

Now roaring, a fire in the womb gives rise to life. And she says resistance to reduction—the fire—is good. This life is very good.

From poetics of pain to prose of potential, this book emerged out of the possibility of sinking at the hands of abuse—combined with enough of a spark and enough of a Love and enough of a Sisterhood—to say "No" when resignation was such a reasonable option. I had not chosen the fight, but it was mine. I could not turn my back on the fight because it was in me. It felt warm because it was alive; it was fueled by anger. Anger at the unjust things— pinpointed on abuse, and violation, and cover-up, and authority used to silence. This anger emerged when abuse threatened life. This anger breeds clarity. I do not need to sink for the violence he perpetrated. This anger is saving. It does good. I am cultivating a relationship with anger because it can be good, and it is necessary for following Jesus in a world with injustice.

Yet, I was taught that anger was bad. It was an unsanctioned emotion that did not belong in the repertoire of a good girl. It was supposed to get weeded out of a Christian life. I was taught that anger itself was wrong—not just that violent acts associated with anger were the wrong or that consuming bitterness related to unexamined anger was the wrong. What I now view as a falsehood accompanied me well into adulthood until I experienced anger as a life-giving force, a gift of redemption and hope.

This anger has not prompted retaliation. What it has done is this. It has risen. It has energized me for the hard work of moving through suffering, and it has oriented me toward working against structural and institutional violence. That orientation put me in contact with women and gender non-conforming community organizers. I was a novice, and I wanted to learn from their skillfulness with anger because I had seen them funnel anger in ways that liberate them as well as communities around them. I discovered wisdom regarding anger, comfort in relationship to anger, and facility in working with anger.

While these organizers taught me to see more in anger than I previously had been allowed to notice, things shifted in me. I became more willing to be a braver version of myself because I could sustain my gaze on offensive occurrences around me without fulfilling the socially conscripted and polite averting of my eyes. Now I can keep seeing a man while he explains his philosophy about the assigned reading, and I can see him, and his good points, and also his bluster that comes from being underprepared. Earlier, I would shrink, thinking, "That's not how I read it. What did I miss?" only later to overhear how glad the man was that the professor had bought his smoke and mirrors. Now I'm learning to sustain my attention to the pain that is caused by structural injustice without needing to protect myself or others from that pain, without resignation, and without flailing as I try to apply as many Band-Aids as possible. Instead, I've gained increased stamina to stay with tense conversations and to abide with the discomfort of recognizing how powerful people benefit mightily from others' pain. Another gaze I can now endure is a prolonged gaze at myself, and I do not need to pantomime perfection to take that close look. I can face off with my lopsided grins, my brush-ups with walls, my cooking-with-Jan ruined batches of what I had imagined as savory goodness but yielded a burnt cream sauce as I tried juggling in three other tasks.

To help facilitate readers taking your own steps toward liberation, I invite you into relationships with Mary Gonzales, Andrea (Drea) Hall, Sue Engh, and Kelly Marciales. These relationships might help liberate us from socially constructed and restrictive understandings of anger—understandings that have often stealthily formed countless people to be nice folx instead of feeling or expressing anger over the causes of human and planetary suffering. Silencing our anger, many of us remain inattentive to and silent about the structural violence of economic disparity, racism, sexism, colonization, and, regretfully, so many other injustices. Instead of numbing out, readers could, if you wish, open yourselves to a process of potential transformation. Readers will be accompanied by women, especially Drea, Sue, Kelly, and Mary, who have taken the long, hard look at themselves and practiced steps toward becoming more powerful. Readers will also be accompanied by choreographers, ethicists, and philosophers—both old and new—so you can consider who benefits from certain people (yourself included) not being angry about injustice. Readers might move toward a happier and more free life through ethical attention to anger and good practices of it. Readers can start thinking more strategically about their own anger or lack thereof and can practice into helping choreograph or coach other people's anger, pointing it in the direction of social good.

Jan Schnell
Solstead (prairie restoration site)
May 25, 2023

Introduction

Some people are ready to think about how anger (mal)functions in your life and how it could do better work for you. This book is for you. This book is for the nuns who are a vibrant heart of the Roman Catholic Church, and who have shared their struggles to find status equity as they invest their daily work and whole lives in a pursuit of justice in Jesus's name. This writing is for Lutheran deacons whose vigor for bridging between church and world radiates such Christ-like vocation, yet who notice that the church that called them has yet to provide well-structured paths for their vocational flourishing. It is for wonderfully Queer Methodist pastors whose hearts remain strangely afire even while the glacial pace of the church froze their calls. It is for community organizers who will recognize the organizing cycle here and enjoy thinking with these mighty organizers about how you choreograph the formation of leaders. Women community organizers take center stage, the binary-skeptic author narrates stories and theories, women theorists drop content, and boundary-crossing stories take pride of place.[1]

Maybe life's done some messy things with you; still, you're determined to embrace life as a flourishing place for you and others. Maybe you want to use every tool there is to bring about good, and anger has remained untapped or counterproductive, and you'd like to see that change. If this content makes you feel like squirming, and you find yourself saying, "Yes, but . . .," yet still feel open, then this book is for you. This book is for you if you're ready for your own or your community's anger to do some good for all. This book is an accompanied guide to notice the good in anger, to reconsider your relationship to anger, and to point that anger toward structural issues as fuel for participation in prosocial, systemic change. Working with anger will not make you angry, but it might make you free.

A quick note on what this book does not do: it will not address anger a person may have toward an individual who caused unjust harm, where that individual needs to be confronted. Anger toward one individual you need to continue to interact with is important, and you may find some skills here that you can apply, but this book doesn't do the good work that psychologists and counselors do. This book shows how to level up personal anger so that it does good for whole communities.

This book wrestles with the ways that anger can be a virtuous emotion that helps people show up well and mightily for their communities. Its overarching question finds a home in the landscape of religious ethics. It calls upon philosophy of emotion and choreographic theory to articulate what it means to experience anger in morally good ways and how virtuous anger can be cultivated.

Sue Engh, Kelly Marciales, Mary Gonzales, and Drea Hall inhabit overlapping lifeworlds; they all have intersected at some point with faith-based organizing training events. Downtown Berkeley, just off the bustling Shattuck Avenue, houses a graduate school on the third floor of an inconspicuous building. Kelly, Mary, and Sue, along with several colleagues, led a week-long community-organizing training. I sat at a desk off to the side, fastidiously taking notes—my way of reveling in their wisdom. Months later in Chicago, Mary, Drea, and Sue were together at a train-the-trainer event. This project began with their insights. Their professional worlds intersect, yet their backgrounds and the main contexts in which they primarily work vary greatly. Mary Gonzales describes herself as a Mexican American woman and a Catholic. Gonzales cofounded the Gamaliel Foundation with her husband, Gregory Galluzzo, founded Gamaliel of California and its affiliates, and created Ntosake—a training program designed by, for, and with women in Gamaliel. Now in her retirement, she mentors young organizers and organizes locally in her community of Pilsen in Chicago. Drea Hall describes herself as an African American who attends a nondenominational and evangelical church. As a social worker, she has been an organizer with the Service

Sue Engh   Kelly Marciales   Mary Gonzales   Drea Hall

Employee International Union and has made life more livable for families and youth through Chicago public schools and the Chicago Coalition for the Homeless. Drea is now chief executive officer (CEO) of MYSI Corporation—a nonprofit child welfare agency that supports youth by providing transitional housing and life-skills programing. Sue Engh describes herself as a white, midwestern, semiretired Lutheran pastor. From 2007 to 2019, she served as the director for congregation-based community organizing for the Evangelical Lutheran Church in America (ELCA), where she strategically built an interreligious, nationwide cohort for people in ministry using the arts of organizing. She is now a consultant, does collaborative writing projects, and helps lead her congregation's antiracism efforts. Kelly Marciales describes herself as a Japanese Irish American and a United Methodist. Marciales was the executive director and lead organizer of Valley Interfaith Action and organized around quality-of-life issues for people in Alaska's Matanuska-Susitna (Mat-Su) Borough when I first met her. Since then, Kelly became the ELCA program coordinator of community organizing and director of the Organizing for Mission Network after Sue retired. Now she serves as the director of Alaska Pacific University's Kellogg campus, a leader in project-based learning programs that address sustainable and socially responsible agriculture and food security in cold-climate areas. Throughout this book, Drea, Sue, Kelly, and Mary, plus some of their colleagues, share their thoughts about both limiting and liberative religious interpretations of anger.[2] They tell their views of what anger is and what it does within community organizing.

RECEIVING THE ORGANIZERS' STORIES

Sue's, Kelly's, Mary's, and Drea's stories shepherd every chapter. Their longer narratives kick off each section of this book. Some readers might want to defy the chronological chapter order and first read the chapters that introduce their stories (chapters 1, 4, 7, and 10) before turning to the rest of the book. That would be another good path. Church leaders, organizers, or those interested in a virtuous relationship with anger may be moved by these women's phronesis—practical wisdom that withstands tests that theories written at desks in ivory towers don't surpass. Their understandings of anger have evolved through tests of time—decades of their lives, political corruption, religious worldviews, human action (and some humans' inaction), and affronts to their and others' hope.

The women's stories are honest, deep, real, and vulnerable. Each of them overcame both interior and imposed limitations on their journeys to become the powerful organizers you are about to meet.[3] Although I attempt to introduce you to these real, embodied powerhouses, they are so much more than I can show here; none of the accounts claims to attend comprehensively to the breadth, depth, and wisdom of these women and their lived experience.

In each of their chapters, there are three consistent parts: the women's social locations, journeys into community organizing, and religious views impacting their perceptions of anger. Regarding religious views, each names church practices and biblical passages that made them think anger must not be good. At the same time, yet conversely, they also show how they grew to cherish biblical stories that showed anger being used well by God and others. Despite being similarly structured, each story differs in style and focus because Kelly, Mary, Drea, and Sue differ significantly from one another—each bringing her own personality and capacities to bear on the vocation of community organizer. Amid all their difference, readers will also see similarities among the women. They make it plain that leaders have moral and professional obligations to be conscious and critical of white dominant culture. In addition, each of them chose at some point to care more about being respected than being liked. Yet, giving up being well liked as a primary goal has put them in precisely the challenging, confrontational, vulnerable, transformational conversations in which they thrive. These conversations have formed lifelong, abiding, authentic connections with many people and communities. In their four chapters, no other voices get to enter because it is all about encountering four change agents whose lives have no shortage of laughter and love and hope.

HOW TO USE THIS BOOK

One aspiration for this project is that readers might be freed to consider their own relationship with anger and goodness. I want to discuss anger in such a way that calls you to fuller selfhood, challenging you to notice how some patterns cost you dearly and betray the strength that you are created to embody. The women's voices might inspire you to cultivate anger into a form that benefits the publics about which you care the most. Recognizing their own stories of pain and success, this book helps readers effectively challenge and extend the work of contemporary academic theoreticians.

You can increase your access to prosocial anger through an intentional and informal cultivation of a love-based anger—agapic anger. An advantage to being able to shape your anger and the movements you want anger to have in your life—movements that maximize your own and your communities' flourishing—is that you become one who can informally help others to transform their anger. This transforms the people themselves as they invest in their own liberation and, as a result, increases potential for social transformation. Let's face it; oppression will continue its insidious masquerade, but if you can raise up anger-informed leaders around you, you will create networks and communities nimble enough to confront each new guise. Then as you watch attentively, you might see a social choreography of sorts that gets enacted in communities of accountability for mutual flourishing.

PART I

Experiencing Anger

Stuffing anger does not work well. Bottled inside, anger feels like chaotic pressure that exacerbates a person's anxiety. There are skillful ways to choreograph anger so it neither gets stuffed and eats at one from the inside out, nor explodes, unwittingly hurting things in its path. Building on the women's stories, chapter 2 names what anger is and identifies varieties of angers to show more nuance within people's experience of anger. The women's stories promote a specific kind of anger, but there are many forms of anger. Some of these they let go—deeming them not worth their effort. Others they choreograph into a form of anger that does the world good.

Chapter 3 makes a case for why anger is crucial for transformation and freedom, and it shows specific places where certain people's exercise of anger is constrained in ways that decrease their agency and limit flourishing. Chapter 1 opens the door to Mary's story to examine why society paves the way for some people's power while restricting others'. Among other unapologetic convictions, she offers, "You should have a phenomenal desire for power, [defined as] the ability to act." Mary's conviction highlights the need to consider where people do or don't experience power. Her conviction calls forth an examination of when to desire power. Mary, based on her being a Spanish-speaking woman, got invited to tamp down her desire to be powerful. That diminishment of agency was inconsistent with her identity and vocation. Mary rejected the invitation to be small; instead, she acts mightily for communal good.

CHAPTER ONE

A Rock in My Pocket

Meet Mary Gonzales

On the day the landlord came, she was playing out front with the other kids. At first glimpse of the landlord, they scattered, streaming toward their little apartments, doors slamming behind vanishing children. Eight-year-old Mary dove into a closet, fearing the landlord would come knocking at the door of the four-room apartment the thirteen of them called home. Her fear was reasonable; just the day before, her mom, Guadalupe Reyes, had reported him to the city because they had no heat in the Chicago cold but did have a brand-new baby at home. He banged on the door. Her mom opened it. Peering through the slit in the cracked-open closet, Mary watched. The landlord flew into her mother's face, screaming at her.

"You and your brood are going to wind up sleeping on the street tonight!" And my father stepped up behind my mother and whispered to her, and I could hear him speaking to her saying, "Don't say anything. Don't start anything." And my mother, very gently she said to him in Spanish, "If you're not going to help me, step back." She turned to the landlord and said, "Go ahead and try it. Just you try it," and she slammed the door in his face.

Two emotions flooded Mary. The first was fear; this was already her second home, the first lying under the paved expanse of the Dan Ryan Expressway. "Am I really gonna sleep on the street tonight? Will I get to take my bed? What will people think if I'm out there sleeping on the street?" The second was excitement. "I had never seen this beautiful, little, tortilla-making, gentle, loving mother turn into a grizzly bear. And I saw a grizzly bear. And I think that day she licensed me—she licensed me to become a grizzly bear, and not necessarily follow my father's lead, which was, 'Be gentle and sweet and soft-spoken.'"

Mary's father, Andres Reyes, whose name Mary consistently accompanies with words like "excellent," "wonderful," "beautiful," responded to his own oppression as an undocumented immigrant working in the fields and later at Wisconsin Steel Works, where he was treated as inferior, by teaching his children to "behave, excel, stay out of trouble, keep your opinions to yourself, and be helpful to others when you can." Mary, the oldest of eleven, learned young how to cook, clean, and mother. The voice of her father, who wanted her life to be easier than his, was in her ear: "Lower your voice. Don't look at anybody eye to eye; it's not respectful."

The first words from her towering kindergarten teacher at William Ray Elementary School in Hyde Park silenced Mary. "No Español." The only brown-skinned child she knew of at her school, Mary recalls not speaking in school for two years. Español was the only language Mary spoke, as her father and her grandmother, who lived with them, spoke only Spanish. Throughout her kindergarten year, Mary figures she exasperated her bilingual mother, pestering her to teach Mary English. "So, she had to work with me every evening teaching me simple phrases, teaching me how to read the book in English, teaching me what this was and what that was—over and over and over. And so, by the time I got to second grade, I was pretty good." For Mary, it was traumatizing: "you're five; no one looks like you; no one speaks like you; you can't look like them; you can't speak like them."

"How do you overcome 'No Español'?" Mary learned that the safe way to speak was in English, and the feminine way to speak was gently and softly. This expectation stirred conflict inside Mary. "I discovered my voice, and it was loud. So, I had a choice: listen to my daddy, who said, 'Lower your voice,' or listen to my heart, which said, 'Raise your voice!' I raised my voice." Already in grade school, Mary decided she'd have to be competitive to be heard and seen. "So, I began to be very competitive academically. I was always at the top of my class. Always, always at the top of my class."

Mary was bound for Hyde Park High School until, just months before junior high graduation, someone described Chicago Vocational High School (CVHS) to her, and it piqued her interest. To her parents, who had "three years of formal education between them," a high school education seemed unnecessary for her probable life of raising kids. Simultaneously, high school was a big deal—maybe like attending graduate school today. Mary's attending was not a given, but her father's remark to her mom, "If you want to send her . . ." was enough, and four years later she graduated top of her class at CVHS with expertise running machines. She got out forty days early to secure a job before the market flooded with new high school grads. By May 1, she had a full-time job working for Marshal Fields in their payroll department.

Mid-June she was back for her high school graduation. Award in one hand, diploma in the other, she consoled her teary-eyed teacher who so desperately wanted Mary to go on to university. But Mary thought differently. "I have to get out and help Dad," who, on a steel-worker's salary, was now supporting a critically diabetic grandfather, brother Bobby, whose bout of spinal meningitis in infancy left him with intense care needs, and the other nine kids still at home along with Guadalupe, who tended to them all. To Mary, this choice was clear. "I got out and went to work. I had several jobs (payroll, accounting, nonprofit secretary, legal secretary) but none of them ever fulfilled me. I did a good job, but they didn't fulfill me."

Mary quit her job as a legal secretary when she had kids, but her husband's opinion regarding her working would vacillate. When she was staying home, "He would always say to me, 'Well, we're never going to get anywhere because I'm the sole support. If you were working, we could stash some money here.' So, I'd get a job and then he'd say, 'Well, now you've abandoned me. Abandoned the children.' So, I quit my job and then he'd say, 'Oh, well, here I am again.'"

By this time Mary's family had moved to Pilsen, a suburb with changing demographics, growing from 20 to 70 percent Hispanic. Mary credits this neighborhood for reteaching her the Spanish language she had been losing and immersing her in beloved community with a sense of belonging and dignity.

WALKING WITH LIONS

By 1967, Mary's parents faced a crisis with Bobby's need for twenty-four-hour care. Mary recalls he was seventeen, big and strong and processing mentally as a five-year-old, so, he, not knowing his own strength, would break things. "So, I was with my mom sitting there trying to figure out 'What are we gonna do? What are we gonna do?' And we're forever calling people—my mother was on the phone all the time and writing letters. Nothing. But in '68 a law is passed in Illinois that says that if a school system cannot provide services for your children, you are entitled to services in a community-based organization. And this man we had never met from Chicago State University came and met us and said, 'I know how to do this.'" Guadalupe and Mary worked with him to apply for a grant and build a neighborhood institution that could provide Bobby with the services guaranteed by this law.

Mary says she didn't know too much about organizing. "I was just a very angry young woman. Very, very angry young woman. I was about twenty-four, twenty-five, so I took on the state for an initial grant. My mother was the leader organizing other neighborhood parents, and I was the one figuring out how to force the political structures. And so, we'd have actions" (collective, public activities designed to promote social change that benefits a certain oppressed population). "She would turn out the people and I was creating the strategy." They got their grant and created Esperanza School,[1] where Bobby went to school for the first time in 1969 when he was nineteen. Very soon, Bobby was too old for Esperanza, and Guadalupe and Mary started over again. By 1972 they had created El Valor, a nonprofit community organization "that strives for a community in which all members, including individuals with special needs, can live, learn and work."[2]

Throughout this time Mary increasingly found herself accompanying her mother to all sorts of community meetings about social concerns in Pilsen: "overcrowded schools, a lot of discrimination on the part of principals, with teachers, of police, garbage overflowing in the alleys . . . So, I begin to listen, and I begin to get a little angry, trying to figure out, 'What can we do? What can we do?'" In 1972, a group of Jesuit seminarians, who would alter Mary's life, arrived from Berkeley to learn how to do community organizing. "And they're all young, and mad as hell, wanting to revolutionize." Although Mary hated so many meetings, "at the same time, I was being drawn to what I felt was an energy. There was a right to be angry; there was a way to solve these things. I was sensing this in what they were saying and what they were doing."

Those seminarians started an action with "a group of parents who complained that the principal of this one school was very cruel to the brown-skinned children." When their collective action resulted in getting a new principal, Mary was amazed what a difference parents could make. Mary realized, "Holy crap! This is what I like to do. There's energy, excitement, a lot of people. So, I started going to all these meetings and next thing you know, I'm the president of the organization."

"And because of that" investment in organizing, "my husband leaves me in 1974. I think he was afraid. He could see changes in me I couldn't see, and I think he was afraid of those. And I think he thought 'She's got a mortgage, five kids, four of them in Catholic schools; she can't make it.' So anyway, he departed, and two days later I didn't know what to do. I needed a job. I had my mother and my disabled brother living downstairs rent free." A priest came to her house and said that she needed a job. "I said, 'I know, but all I know how to do is type and run office machines. I don't know how to do anything else. I can't make enough money to pay the mortgage.'" The next afternoon the priest was back with another parish member. All afternoon the three of them wrote a resume, typed, printed, and mailed a hundred copies. Within a week, she had a job. "I used to think if I could just earn $8,000. $8,000! I think I can make it at $8,000 a year. And I get a job at $14,000!" She became the director of a small program inside a large social service agency and began to value long-term stability, thinking, "'I'll do organizing in here. Maybe not at the extent that I was doing out there, but I'll do organizing inside this place, and I'll become vested in a pension plan.' So, I remained five years, six years, and I now have sixty-five people working under me and I'm thinking, 'I'm doing pretty damn good, right?'"

By then the seminarians had gone back to the West Coast. Mary and her friend Greg, now a Jesuit priest, "would get on the phone and argue about organizing, and he'd tell me what he was doing."

And I'd say, "Well, that sounds like crap. Why don't you do something that's real?" And then he'd say, "Well, when are you going to give up that stupid job and go into organizing?" And I'd say, "You know what? I don't want to talk to anyone." So, we were friends.

Greg came to Mary's sister's wedding years later, bringing his mother, sister, and another priest. "And the next day he comes over to visit with us, and with my mom and all my kids. Everyone goes to bed, and we sat at my kitchen table, drinking a glass of wine and just talking and talking and talking. So, the next morning he leaves. They all come to say goodbye—his sister, mother, and the priest. Then we're on the phone for two weeks, probably two hours a night, just talking about whether we were more than friends. By the end of the conversation, we decided he has to leave the Jesuits; I have to get a divorce—'cause I never had—I never got divorced. So, I married Greg a year later, and we started Gamaliel. So that's when I entered [organizing] professionally."

The Gamaliel National Network now has a presence in seventeen states with seven state-wide offices and forty-four affiliates.[3] "Gamaliel was just inching along; [Greg, its CEO] was making $12,000 a year—and maybe $10,000. I had low salaries, long work weeks, and happiness. I spent my life just working as an organizer, and I loved it because I was free."

Mary noticed women wanted a different sort of training, so she began running a "Women's Weekend," which evolved into Ntosake, a women's training program within Gamaliel. "We found that women hungered to find new and powerful ways to transform their lives. This weekend was conceived as an opportunity for women to freely explore building a life as a leader in their communities and congregations."[4] In the closing sermon for a women's training, Reverend Brenda Hayes of the African Methodist Episcopal Church used the term *ntosake* as a central image. The name comes from the South African word *ntosake* which means "[s]he who walks with lions; she who carries her own things." This word struck a chord with the women gathered. "Upon hearing the word and its definition, an awakening swept through the room and seventy-five women declared, 'We are Ntosake.'"[5]

Mary's stamina is evident; she worked to become simultaneously "looked up to by everyone and feared by everyone." She was forced to take a close look at how she viewed her life story.

> They were saying to me, "You could be great!" And I kept saying, "I just went to high school. I don't know anything. And I went to a vocational school and I learned to type. I'm a fast typist." And they'd say, "No, you're much more than that." I knew who I wanted to be. I wanted to be the best organizer in Gamaliel.

When Gamaliel was about five or six years old, word got around "that the only reason I had a job was that I was married to Gregory Galluzo, who was the CEO. That was the word—because I'm a woman and I'm brown. Who could expect more from me?"

"So, I set out on a mission, and here was my mission: I was going to out-produce every organizer who sat at the table with me. So, if it was national training, I was going to outproduce them. If it was a public action, mine was going to be meaner and tougher and engage more leaders. No matter what it was—I was going to get more press, I was going to get more people, I was going to deliver larger, etc."

"I had to prove to everybody I'm just as good as you are; in fact, I'm better at what I do. It doesn't mean I'm as well educated as you are, but I've got more guts than you have. I've got more stamina than you have. I've got more courage than you have. I've got more vision than you have. I'm angry as hell. Much angrier than you are." Mary has had to face anger—her own and others'—and has determined that a certain form of anger is necessary for a good organizer.

MEETING A REVOLUTIONARY JESUS

On the one hand, the church can be a source of frustration—or even anger—for Mary. "I raised four daughters, and I wanted them to grow up in the faith, but I said to them, 'The only way you're going to survive it is you've got to ignore the priest, the bishop, and the pope. Because they're going to say things that are going to make you feel like you're in the wrong place, but you're NOT in the wrong place.' I've struggled a lot with [the church] and the way I survived it is I've said, 'No one is gonna separate me from my faith.'" While organized religion may cause Mary some consternation, she has grown to understand biblical stories as testifying to Jesus's just action in the world. Seeing Jesus as one who agitated and trained leaders, wielded power and even anger, Mary recognizes her work in organizing as a faith-filled vocation.

Mary detected a revolutionary Jesus in texts she'd been taught to read as tame and sweet. It was the Jesuit priests who held space for Mary to challenge her domesticated view of Jesus. A Roman Catholic, Mary grew up going "to church as a habit as a child, and even as a young adult. I just grew up in a habit. And so, I just did it." For a time, she fell away from the practice of attending worship. Around the neighborhood, she'd bump into her priest, who was warm and welcoming, "but it still wasn't something I was passionate to do. But then organizing happened—and these Jesuits, one in particular whose name was John."

John would come to the house and say, "Do you have a Bible?"

"Yeah, I've got one." And I'd go pull it out.

And he'd sit around talking to me, and he began to describe to me
Jesus as a revolutionary.

"What do you mean? What do you mean?"

Once Mary began to see Jesus differently and identify with him as a change maker, the Bible became clearer and more interesting. She kept picking it up to read.

And then one day I said to Greg, "Was the blessed mother a virgin?"
And he was a very young organizer. And he was reading the
newspaper.

"I don't know."

He wasn't even listening to me. And again, I said, "Greg, was the blessed
mother a virgin?" And he said to me, "How are babies made?" I
pointedly said, "I know how babies are made! I'm asking you a
specific question about what we're taught as Roman Catholics. Was
the blessed mother a virgin?" He said, "How are babies made?" And
I got very irritated. And he said, "Mary, don't get irritated. The way
babies are made today is the way babies were made then."

"Then she's not a virgin."

"Well," he said, "Let's assume she wasn't. Does it shake your faith?
Does it matter to you if she's a virgin or not?"

I said, "No."

He said, "Well, babies were made the same way then as they're made
now."

"Then why is she called a virgin?"

"If you understand the history of the church, in those days, if you
wanted to honor someone, you would say he must have been born
of a virgin. And the church just incorporated it. The church has
incorporated many things in their history."

"So, the hocus pocus—slowly with these men, they were all Jesuits—began to disappear. And suddenly Christ became this angry, kick ass, take-no-prisoners kind of being. He was no longer petting lambs and loving babies and sacrificing, which is exactly what we [had been] trained to be—just like him. And I said, 'No! He trained leaders. He did propositions around self-interest.

He agitated people. He confronted. He went after people and he said, 'This is where the power is. It's with God.'"

"And suddenly I thought, 'Why do I sit in the last pew? I think I'll move up.' So, I began to move up, slowly but surely, until I was up in the front of the church so that I could participate and listen. And I became more critical of what was being said from the pulpit. So, I think the more the cobwebs were taken away from me, it became easier for me to say, 'I could believe this. I don't believe the hocus pocus, but I believe this.'"

Mary takes her transformed biblical interpretation into community organizing trainings. She asks trainees, "How should faith direct people?" She insists that faith cannot just look backward and rehearse past stories; faith has to be forward-looking. "It's so much easier just to tell victim stories because you can raise money. You can sing 'Kumbaya.' You can say, 'I spent my life on the side of the poor. Am I not wonderful? Do I not deserve entry into heaven because I stood with the poor?' Well, that's a bunch of bullshit. So, if you really have a set of values and a faith tradition that's important to you, then you say, 'How am I going to make this real?—Real in the real world; not in heaven, but right here.'" For Mary, faith and values constitute the bedrock in which anger is grounded. "You should have a phenomenal desire for power, the ability to act, so that your anger can be expressed in the world—anger rooted in values and rooted in faith."

Mary sees anger as necessary for people living out their faith, so she stresses the transformation necessary to move from simply thinking about justice or doing one-off direct service projects to enacting justice that transforms systems. She questioned a room full of people training to become trainers. "How do you move a group of people from being good people who believe in justice, who want to see change, who pray about it . . . to understand that God works through us—uses our hands and our feet and our minds in order to make change in this world? God's not going to come down and do magic tricks. God's gonna depend on you and me to make the changes that need to be made. Number one, you've got to be ready to move someone from the position of saying, 'I'm a good person and I just want to do just work' to someone who says, 'Well, maybe I am somewhat responsible here. I have to assume a position of taking power. I have to build my own power base. I have to figure out why I want it. I have to figure out how I'm gonna remove the obstacles that get in my way.'"

CHAPTER TWO

Naming Anger

The Evolution of a Definition

Anger is a response to the unjust violation of a value. This definition differs from that taught to many people. Nevertheless, this definition is consistent with the philosophy of emotion, and it helps people to consider anger without situating it as negative from the start.

Anger can mean a lot of different things to a lot of people. Sue is succinct. "Anger is the legitimate reaction to the violation of a value." Drea says that "anger is a feeling. I think it's internal. It can be impacted by external factors, but it's something that's within you. It's created by feelings of disappointment, places of injustice, things of sadness. It can be a negative feeling, and it can lead to bad things depending on how you handle your anger. I think in organizing we sometimes help people who are very angry about social justice issues with how to manage that anger."

Kelly's understanding of anger changed over her lifetime because she grew up with anger being culturally unacceptable, especially for women and younger generations. "The impact of negative associations with anger has been a slow process to grow into an understanding of the importance of anger in relationships and in civic life." Although it was difficult to shift inherited, childhood connotations of an emotion, Kelly has come to think that "anger is not a forbidden sin but an expression of disapproval of injustice and a tool that binds communities together against regimes, monarchies, idolatry, false nationalism, sexism, racism, and other systemic injustices that permeate our lives." Reflecting on her current definition of anger, Kelly says, "I could not have realized this earlier because it was a slow turn to get oriented rightly, but now I have the privilege of teaching my four children what I see now so they can begin life oriented toward justice."

For Mary, "It's an expression of who you are. It's an expression of the courage you have; it's an expression of what you value; it's an expression of an attitude you have about life." An expression of identity, courage, value, and life outlook describes a particular form of anger that Mary regards as worth engaging. When she clarifies the kind of anger she is thinking of, her words are akin to those of Sue and Kelly: "We're talking about a justified anger that's rooted in the violation of something you value."

Understandings of what anger is have evolved throughout human history. During antiquity, Aristotle named anger as a form of being moved by what a person perceives to be an unjust harm, perpetrated against herself or someone for whom she cares, where the person perceives the removal of the harm to be very important but also difficult.[1] Current neuroscience shows that anger is instinctual in the bodies of humans and animals alike. Offenses people experience evoke physiological reactions because of neurological responses concentrated in the left frontal lobe of the brain. Therefore, anger unavoidably will occur in people.

Neuroscientific research also suggests that emotions, including anger, are changes in the autonomic nervous system, which regulates muscles, organs, and biochemicals.[2] Researchers Ralph Adolphs and David J. Anderson find that emotions directly influence bodily and cognitive processes that account for behavior, attention, and memory.[3] These research findings both are and are not new. Philosophers of emotion noticed physiological aspects of anger before neuroscience emerged as an explicit discipline. Theologian Thomas Aquinas, speaking from the thirteenth century, says, "[I]t is natural to everything to rise up against things contrary and hurtful" in order to be protected.[4] Neuroscience expands and fine tunes what is known about our body's regulatory system. From a biological perspective, Martin Reuter, with his research team, confirms that "anger is one of the basic emotions inherent in animals and in humans across all ethnical groups."[5] Anger, as instinct, includes a mostly involuntary surge of energy that is caused in many animals, including humans, by a sensory input of an unfair slight.

There is also an evolutionary perspective on what anger is. Initial surges of anger resemble reflexes. Adolphs and Anderson argue convincingly in *The Neuroscience of Emotion* that "emotions may have evolved out of reflexes," which are "narrow, and automatic stimulus-response mapping[s]." With reflexes, a stimulus triggers an involuntary response experienced within the body.[6] Reflexes are limited by a short duration and low adaptability, but the emotions that build on them "show properties that go well beyond what reflexes can accomplish."[7] Emotions may have evolved from more primitive reflexes because animals needed more flexibility in their responses to sensory inputs because reflexes were "too narrowly tuned to specific stimuli, and too rigid and uncontrollable in how they cause behaviors."[8] Adolphs and Anderson give the example of disgust, which they say arose as a reflex to avoid contamination and evolved as an emotion, through learning, to include more complex needs for social regulation. Adolphs and Anderson say that, in disgust, both innate and learned aspects remain. Anger likewise retains certain aspects that are automatic and impulsive, which can be very difficult to change because they erupt like reflexes.

Given these biological roots, angry impulses just do occur periodically in most healthy animals, including humans. However, at least in humans, anger also has aspects that are generated more through cultural conditioning and personal experience, which can be shaped with thoughtfulness over time. Drawing then from the women, Aristotle, and neurobiology, our shorthand definition of anger is a bodily response to the violation of a value.

MULTIPLE FORMS OF ANGER

The way our culture talks about anger makes it seem like it's just one thing. In actuality, anger comes in many varieties—a key insight that allows for choosing one form while not assenting to others. Kelly, Mary, Sue, and Drea were aware of fluid angers. The women have identified some anger to which they assent and may even cautiously laud; at the same time, they resist and denounce other angers they deem opposed to people's well-being or the health of vulnerable communities. Mary recognizes that she experiences forms of anger that are more or less beneficial to her and her communities. In a conversation among organizers, Mary pointedly asks another organizer, "Are you in control of your anger? . . . Does it just happen, or do you bring it out?" The question gets put back to Mary, who says, "Well, I think that maybe once or twice a year my anger will just jump out at something that instantaneously happens and I just react. But most of the time it's a strategic decision to use it." She has put her finger on one sort of anger that just erupts—an instantaneous reaction—and another form of anger that she consciously accesses and uses.

Drea also notices a kind of anger that bursts forth. "When I have bad anger—which of course I still have and which is usually about injustice, but just not handled the right way"—that anger is "just real quick, just feeling." She offers this example of quick anger that is counter to the kind she tries to cultivate. "So, I was driving by a Bulls game, and it was at night, and there were some drunk guys. We had a green light, [but] a couple of them got in the street and started saying, 'Fuck you,' called me a bitch. And normally I'd just be like, 'They're drunk dudes; whatever.' But I got mad because I'm tired of these men—or even white people—disrespecting. And I swung my jeep back around and I pull up on them." They were taken off guard. "And I'm like, 'Listen, you don't even know who you're talking to. . . . Just watch it.'" This is a kind of anger she wants to coach herself to act on less, so afterward "I debrief the situation" with a trusted friend, family member, or colleague, talking through what happened and wondering about better paths.

Pamela, an organizer, trainer, and long-term colleague of Mary and Sue, says, "I feel like we need different words for different kinds of anger. There's genuine anger—when any of us talk about using anger as a tool in agitations or conversations—and that's qualitatively different than [the] manufactured outrage" generated by various media in the United States. Pamela goes on to distinguish between many forms of anger—some that give credibility and others that reduce credibility. "What I like about the kind of training we do, is we give people permission and encouragement to get angry—not like rageful. I think a lot of people, when they think about anger, they think about . . ." Mary joins in: "going and hitting someone . . ." Pamela continues, "Yeah . . . like throwing things and rage. And that's not what we're talking about. But we *are* talking about—you get to *feel* angry. It's a natural human thing, and no one should be telling you that you're not allowed to do that."

Pamela, similar to Mary and Drea, notices at least two kinds of anger: one that is "not what we're talking about"—a kind that turns, for example, to violence—and another form that is indispensable because it alerts people to what's happening within them and can fuel strategic action. Still, the fact that people need "permission and encouragement to get angry" indicates that even this promoted sort of anger is somewhat culturally shunned.

Drea points out that anger has various levels and can be oriented in more or less helpful directions. "I meet people where they're at. I want to know, 'To what level are you angry?' You're angry to the point of no communication?—then I'm probably not gonna mess with [invest in] you. But if you're angry to the point where you're willing to listen, and here's a solution!—you've gotta be solution-orientated if you want to address your anger. I'm open to people being angry with hopes that they would turn it into a solution-focused type of strategy. So I don't shy away from anger."

While the women resist culturally conditioned and blanket demonization of all anger, they've come up with their own informal set of principles by which they judge whether an anger is worth their energy. But it is complicated. Even something that may seem as straightforward as avoiding the desire for revenge has finely grained nuances when it plays out on the street. Mary commends certain experiences of anger in her life that appear to involve a desire for payback.

Starting her story facetiously, Mary says, "My father died at the ripe old age of sixty-two." She explains, "He was a steel worker—a chipper. Standing right over those hot ovens as the hot steel was coming out and he had to chip off that black crud with that little power hammer. What was he swallowing all day? Steel dust—all day long, because I could smell it on him at the dinner table. But he never missed a day of work—was proud of his job. He was just a great worker until he died of two very large, malignant tumors in the brain. Where did he get them? Swallowing that steel dust."

"Before he died, he said to me, 'Don't worry, I worked thirty years in this plant. I've got a pension plan. Your little brothers and sisters—there were still six at home—are going to be fine, and so is your mother. Don't worry. Go to the plant; talk to this guy; he will help you.' And I took my mother to the plant, and my mother got his pension—$47.50 a month for the rest of her life for six children and her [far less cushion than her father had believed]. How did I feel? How did I feel? I was outraged. It created so much stress. I was a young adult; I was married already; I was having children. I had siblings of all ages—teenagers and in high school, some just getting out of high school. It was poverty from the bottom all the way to the top, so we had several difficult years. But I said, 'Somebody's gonna pay. Somebody's gonna pay. Somebody's gonna pay.'"

Mary's "gonna pay" comment sounds like a desire for payback. Neo-Stoic ethicist Martha Nussbaum says anger's characteristic feature of envisioning payback amounts to magical thinking that what one lost when slighted (e.g., reputation, status, financial security) might be recovered.[9] Regarding Mary's experience, Nussbaum might say that it would be irrational to imagine that the steel company's fair remuneration of the family could account for the profound injustice of her dad's working conditions and loss of life.

Nussbaum deems it reasonable to be upset by violation a friend suffers but urges people to keep their focus on the friend—on benefitting her or making constructive social changes on behalf of the good of society—rather than focusing on the violator and beginning to fantasize about causing him reciprocal pain. Nussbaum holds that there is in fact no way that causing the wrongdoer pain could restore what has been lost. It could only generate more pain. The best emotional response, per Nussbaum, is one that does not indulge the desire for payback. Nussbaum writes, "I am inclined to see [anger at the violation of a friend] as a type of morally inflected compassion," and not anger at all—not involving a desire for payback.[10] In contrast to Nussbaum, even though the women also may be leery about payback-anger, they do not shy away from calling their emotional response to injustice "anger."

When Mary says, "So I've spent my life evening the score," she is not entertaining magical thinking. Mary recognizes that fixating on the steel company is a misuse of her valuable time, especially when there is no expectation that the company could atone for the damages it caused her family. She does not anticipate pleasure in paying the steel company back, pain for pain. Instead, she looks for places where her anger could, in her words, "pay off." She transfers her anger about her dad's working conditions, death, and non-life-sustaining pension forward; she pays her anger over the steel plant forward to benefit future people.

Mary wants to experience a payoff in her anger by applying it to a worthwhile end. "You've got to get in touch with your own life story, and you've got to know why the hell you're so pissed off. You have to figure out why you're so pissed off and begin to use that anger. And if there's no payoff for you, why the hell would you invest your emotion, your pain—the everything that comes with anger, right?!" Her jaw is set, she faces ahead, and she harnesses her anger in order to invest it in the future. Mary's anger that pays off in ways that benefit communities differs from what Nussbaum identified as payback-anger. Mary's is a nuanced, expansive, non-vengeful view of what "evening the score" can mean; it reinforces the notion of multiple forms of anger.

Theorists echo what the women have witnessed: anger comes in a variety of forms.[11] Not all forms involve the desire for vengeance. Three of several possible species of anger include payback-anger, protection-anger, and recognition-anger. While payback-anger could rightly be said to include a desire for vengeance, neither protection- nor recognition-anger would be well characterized as including a desire for vengeance. Protection-anger is a desire to restrain an offender's ability to do harm when there is imminent danger of injury to oneself or a loved one, and recognition-anger "names a desire to make someone acknowledge our equal human dignity or the dignity of others for whom we care."[12]

Aquinas also thinks that there are multiple species of anger.[13] Aquinas calls κόλος (kolos) "the *first* species of anger" that is quickly aroused.[14] He points to three additional, specific forms of anger by name. *Furor* is an explosive anger akin to the anger that, in Mary's experience, sometimes just jumps out. *Fel* refers to a bilious anger that may play a role in the manufactured outrage of which Pamela Twiss spoke previously. Finally, *minor* is a simmering, menacing anger like what Mary and Pamela referred to in their back-and-forth—an anger that builds up over time and can result in hitting someone or throwing things. These three were all forms the women cautioned against enacting; yet, they find agapic anger worth giving people permission and encouragement to express. As heard from Sue, such anger is a "legitimate reaction to the violation of a value." Agapic anger is a response to an unjust harm—a response that translates the harm to its communal level by examining its systemic causes and finding energy to confront and take steps toward structural transformation.[15]

THE PRESENCE OF VENGEANCE

Many philosophers, especially Stoics (e.g., Seneca) and neo-Stoics (e.g., Nussbaum), argue that vengeance or payback is part of the basic definition of anger. Even Aquinas, in his Aristotelian virtue ethics, defines anger as "a desire for *vindicta*."[16] Yet, there are forms of anger that are not vengeful or vindictive. There are forms of anger that do not have what theorists often consider anger's defining quality.

For example, the women's experiences of non-vengeful anger are still anger. This can be difficult to see since philosophers have tended to use the word *vindicta* (often translated as "vengeance") to describe anger. However, the term *vindicta* cannot uniformly be translated as "vengeance." For example, Aquinas views *vindicta* as good so far as it coheres with justice. "[O]n a Thomistic account, anger is well-described as a predominantly sensory desire for vindi-cation in the wake of an injury that strikes a person as unfair and damaging to her life prospects."[17] Aquinas's meaning of *vindicta* can be described as a form of "vindication" that amends justly for a perpetrated wrong. *Vindicta* is firmly tied to justice in Aquinas's account. Anger "seeks *vindicta* in so far as it seems just. Justice oriented *vindicta* is taken [or exacted] only for that which is done unjustly; hence that which provokes anger is always something considered in the light of an injustice."[18]

In their article "Rethinking Anger," Cates and Schnell affirm that *vindicta* might present with very different goals: legal punishment, the offender becoming mindful of the damage done, the offender acknowledging something valuable they had failed to recognize about the injured person, standing up for oneself, protecting oneself or others about whom one cares, and asserting one's human dignity.[19] While a person might call all of these goals "*vindicta*," the narrower term "vengeance" would be an inaccurate term for many of them. Vengeance as understood in the United States today has too narrow and negative a denotation to rightly capture the desires that comprise multiple forms of angers.

The latitude in Aquinas's meaning of *vindicta* is crucial. So, yes, *vindicta* in Aquinas's view is ultimately a good aim because it rights a wrong. At the same time, there is plenty of room for *vindicta* to go awry, therefore becoming unjust. Aquinas says *vindicta* is sought insofar as it seems just. Yet, what seems just depends on apprehension and judgment, either of which can be more or less apt. In addition, *vindicta* misses the mark when, in aiming at punishment, it metes out more severe punishment than matches the injury.

Vengeance may be one form of the more expansive term *vindicta*. Likewise, a desire for vengeance may constitute part of some forms of anger. However, it is possible to cultivate a form of anger that usually excludes the desire for vengeance or payback. Even when some element of payback remains, anger can be translated into a prosocial desire for just transformation.

Researcher J. Haidt writes, "Anger is perhaps the most underappreciated moral emotion. For every spectacular display of angry violence, there are many more mundane cases of people indignantly standing up for what is right or angrily demanding justice for themselves or others."[20] A certain anger is needed for good living—both in the sense of happiness and of ethics. The community organizers have clarity about the very specific form of anger to which they assent. Agapic anger, as mentioned before, is a response to an unjust harm that translates the harm to its communal level by examining its structural causes and moving with energy to resist sources of that harm.

ANGER DOES GOOD

Stock phrases like "Don't be angry" and "Your anger will do you no good" may roll off the tongue. Biblical passages like "Do not let the sun go down on your anger" (Ephesians 4:26) and "Refrain from anger and forsake wrath" (Psalm 37:8) can have a familiar ring. Such well-known phrases inscribe a cultural norm to which it is easiest to acquiesce. There is a largely unexamined pressure operating in US culture to get rid of anger in one's life as though that is the right thing to do or a path toward happiness. However, getting controlled by a *carte-blanche* discouragement of all anger can blunt people's awareness to God's call for solidarity.

The women's practical wisdom offers an important corrective to people who were taught to view anger as merely morally problematic and something to weed out of religious lives. In these women's experiences, it is morally problematic to relegate anger to a forbidden or unsanctioned corner of their lives. Not being capable of working with a specific sort of anger runs too high a risk of further subverting the course of justice. Drea notes that she feels apprehensive when people aren't angry about awful things. "Actually, when I'm organizing, when people aren't angry that makes me feel uncomfortable—we're talking about babies dying!" If a person's not angry about blatant injustice when working with children's welfare and housing security, "that makes me question you more." Anger is necessary for healthy living that cares for all creation, others, and self.

The time is ripe to reconsider the need for an anger that does good. From overlapping yet distinct perspectives—history, gun violence, and climate change—reports surface that the United States is facing a time of crisis in which underlying structural causes of crises need to be examined and addressed.[21] Furthermore, people in the United States who are critical of systemic injustices cannot and will not wait any longer. As Martin Luther King Jr. wrote, "For years now, I have heard the word 'Wait!' . . . This 'Wait' has almost always meant 'Never.' We must come to see, with one of our distinguished jurists, that 'justice too long delayed is justice denied.'"[22] The time is right to expand the pool of people competent to criticize injustices like racism, sexism, gender binaries, heteronormativity, the maintenance of cycles of poverty, and so on. These critiques and more are underway, but being underway is not sufficient for those who demand justice. If coming to terms with anger is one way to advance the cause of justice, then the concept of anger deserves further analysis and ethical scrutiny so that the wheat of anger is less often thrown out with the chaff.

Here's the thing: people already have anger. It is unrealistic to suppose people might get to choose a life without anger. Mary and the other organizers believe anger is already present in the lives of the people they train but is lacking in focus and efficacy. Sue, Mary, Kelly, and Drea do not try to generate anger in people. Rather, they make space for people's already existent anger to come forward so the person can see it for themselves.

The women also do not manufacture or pretend their own anger. Mary will use stories to remind herself about injustices. Through active recall, Mary is not pretending to be angry. She is remembering or reexperiencing anger in order to attain the appropriate disposition to achieve change. In reliving anger, she exposes herself again to authentic sensory anger—as real as the ongoing injustices of racism, poverty, sexism, and so on, that provoked the anger and as genuine as the liberation toward which her anger points her.

Choreographer Randy Martin exposes a false dichotomy between stillness and action because, from the perspective of dance theorists, bodies in motion are the natural baseline.

> When politics is treated merely as an idea or ideology, it occurs in stillness, awaiting something that will bring people to action or mobilize them. But this presumed gap between a thinking mind and an acting body makes it impossible to understand how people move from a passive to an active state. The presumption of bodies already in motion, what dance takes as a normative condition, could bridge the various splits between mind and body, subject and object, and process and structure that have been so difficult for understandings of social life to negotiate.[23]

The women, too, understand that anger is already alive and in motion in people's daily existence. It is already in some way driving their actions. The organizers' work then is not so much to make people act as to accompany and guide people as they uncover and clarify their own reasons for action.

Mary says, "People are angry. They already are. But they've not the license to use it—to think about it—to express it." She says anger is already present because "it's rooted in real life experiences. It comes out of a life of a million stories, right?! And unless you get in touch with all of that, you can't appreciate the depth of your own life experiences. But anger, anger comes out of your entire life. So that's how I love it because it expresses who I've been for seventy-seven years." Mary recognizes that people's life experiences amass anger; she welcomes people to deal intentionally and well with that anger. Pamela said that as you invest in knowing people and raising up leaders, you end up with "hundreds and hundreds of people's stories." Anger is not only present through one's own life experiences but also through loving and listening to others' stories. The women respect the reality of anger, considering it present before and beyond their training and a beneficial part of the Christian life, since it can facilitate the good that communities need.

Humans need good anger. Writer for *New York* magazine Rebecca Traister observes that anger helps change unjust systems. Traister writes specifically of women's anger because she has experienced and noticed that people tend to receive women's anger differently from men's. Women's rage, she writes, has been systematically disincentivized, diminished, and "has rarely been acknowledged as righteous and patriotic."[24] A form of anger that has rarely been celebrated and has often been erased or reprimanded is an anger with which US women have led social movements for political change. Traister sees a particular kind of women's anger as good because it is key to women's social standing and ability to influence systems. She recognizes such agency as a catalyst for needed social change. In addition, Traister notices that women's anger has other personal benefits. "While I was pouring . . . all of my anger . . . into this [book] project," she says, "I realized that I had begun to sleep well and deeply at night; I had wanted to exercise more than I ever had before. My appetite was healthy; I was communicating well with the people I loved, I was having great sex. . . . there had been something about spending my days and nights immersed in anger—mine and others—that had been undeniably good for me."[25]

Others are also affirming the need for good anger. Virtue ethicist J. Giles Milhaven makes the case that anger is basically good because at its root is a quest for justice.[26] Writer on US women's anger and media critic Soraya Chemaly claims that anger is necessary and beneficial as "one of the most hopeful and forward thinking of all our emotions. It begets transformation, manifesting our passion *and* keeping us invested in the world. . . . It bridges the divide between what 'is' and what 'ought' to be, between a difficult past and improved possibilities. Anger warns us viscerally of violation, threat, and insult."[27] The community organizers agree that cultivating a certain kind of anger is a key element of constructive work toward justice in the form of social transformation.

Social transformation means change that operates on the communal level, aiming at and furthering shared human flourishing. Shared flourishing names the active enjoyment of the most good possible by the largest number of people possible, where everyone takes a personal moral interest in the well-being of everyone else. In a world of grave inequities, such as oppression and poverty, the goal of shared flourishing concerns, first and preferentially, the poor and oppressed. Social transformation tends not to involve an immediate fix of *one* person's temporary problem, which could occur again tomorrow, but tends instead to target the underlying structural causes of problems that perpetuate the suffering of vulnerable people. Structured social practices have the capacity to augment or limit the flourishing of whole populations, and coordinated changes in social practices can lead to more just societies. In addition to Traister, Milhaven, and Chemaly, the women remind each other to stay engaged, remain mad at injustice, and refuse to accept those voices that beckon one to move on quietly without disrupting the status quo. Along with the women, others can increase their capacity to shape morally appropriate anger in order to defy structures of oppression.

CHAPTER THREE

Experiences with Anger

Supremacist, Ecclesial, and Gendered

Anger is experienced quite differently within various groups in the United States. Since anger is tied to the ability to pursue justice, ways society delegitimizes the anger of certain people is a particularly insidious form of inequality and control. Unequal suppression of anger can masquerade in supremacist, ecclesial, and gendered guises. Suppression of anger has been used as a tool of white supremacy, as has been shown by women of color. Within the church, inconsistencies in how anger is understood can curtail women's agency. In US culture women and gender-diverse people face specific pressures and challenges related to the exercise of anger.

A TOOL OF WHITE SUPREMACY

Foreclosing the possibility of good anger has been used as a tool of European colonization and white supremacy. Policy scientist Hema Georgina Biswas writes:

> Colonialism stems from a place of domination . . . [where] "supremacy" justifies subjugation of "inferior beings and territories" and this becomes a representation of a worldview known as imperialism. . . . The effects of imperialism and colonialism leads to the institutionalization of white supremacy.[1]

Biswas suggests colonization stems from an imperialistic worldview; together colonization and imperialism instantiate structures of white supremacy. In order to make it harder to fight against colonialism's domination of lands and white supremacy's domination of people, the anger from certain groups of people has been deemed improper. When anger becomes looked down on as less dignified, less intelligent, and less desirable, then not being angry becomes honorable—that is, morally superior.

Black feminist and cultural critic bell hooks names the repression of anger as a colonizing tool of white supremacy. "I grew up in the apartheid South. We learned when we were very little that black people could die from feeling rage and expressing it to the wrong white folks."[2] In *Killing Rage: Ending Racism*, she says that white people in the United States continued white supremacy by colonizing black Americans. Part of that perpetuation was to teach Black people to repress their rage and not make white people the targets of their anger about racism.[3]

> Most folks associate black rage with the underclass, with desperate and despairing black youth who in their hopelessness feel no need to silence unwanted passions. Those of us black folks who have "made it" have for the most part become skilled at repressing our rage. We do what Ann Petry's heroine tells us we must in that prophetic forties novel about black female rage *The Street*. It is Lutie Johnson who exposes the rage underneath the calm persona. She declares: "Everyday we are choking down that rage." . . . [Psychologists named rage] pathological, explained it away. They did not urge the larger culture to see black rage as something other than sickness, to see it as a potentially healthy, potentially healing response to oppression and exploitation.[4]

The psychological approach to anger appears to treat one person on account of her struggle. A doctor treating a patient's anger, especially in the US diagnosis culture, can give the impression that anger is individual or pathological. Black rage is an explicitly communal, healthy, healing response to oppression. As a collective response that could challenge exploitative authorities, anger gets feared by those who would dominate people groups.

Therefore, it can be convenient for dominant US social and political systems when people evaluate anger as a personal problem instead of as a valid response to social injustice. Scholar of rhetoric Lester Olson, who studies the poetry and activism of Audre Lorde, thinks cultural conditioning dampens women's anger not only at the site of particular people but also in the consciousness of social perceptions of anger. Social linguistic patterns quickly label US women's and Queer anger as "overly emotional" in order to discount their anger.

In the United States, anger is routinely situated in public life as psychological. Consequently, justifiable anger concerning systemic injustice can be displaced into each person's attitude or sensibility. Myths encouraging individualism habituate many people to collude in anger's dis-location from public life into private malady. Characterized as merely personal, anger may be mis-recognized as a maladjusted individual, not a malfunctioning culture that rational people ought to experience with outrage. In this view, what becomes necessary is therapy, not social and political change.[5]

The sleight of hand that Olson identifies treats anger as a psychological sensibility and sidelines prosocial expressions of anger. Behavioral ethicist Sheldene Simola agrees that there are "dominant social perspectives in which anger is negatively construed as a socially inappropriate and irrational dysfunction that is problematic."[6] So prevalent is the notion that anger is a personal problem in need of social constraint that people seek to extinguish anger instead of dismantling white supremacy by which people are rightly incensed.

The politics of invalidating anger at societal levels are exacerbated in the presence of intersectionalities. Philosopher Myisha Cherry notes that, as a Black woman, her anger has not been treated as a normal response to a wrong; instead, she has been treated as wrong for expressing anger.

> As a woman we are expected to express "womanly" emotions. We're expected to be loving, to be compassionate. To express anger is to be perceived as "overly emotional," "irrational," or worse "a female dog." As a black woman, I am stereotypically viewed as "the angry black woman who always has an attitude." My anger is always considered inappropriate.[7]

Cherry adds that a person's social-economic status, race, and gender guide which emotions are socially acceptable.

In *Sister Outsider*, Lorde suggests the "mythic norm" is "white, thin, male, young, heterosexual, Christian, and financially secure."[8] Fitting within this norm comes with privileges such as the right to be angry in public. Author Jess Zimmerman notes that "anger in particular is more stingily restricted the darker you are."[9] If some of these norms do not describe a person's identity, then their expressed anger, although reasonable in light of intersectional oppressions, likely may lead to labels such as unhinged, out of control, or uncivilized.

Amia Srinivasan, philosopher and professor of social and political theory at the University of Oxford, agrees with the immunity that mythic norms afford people as she develops her views on problematic silencing of anger. She shows how "a long philosophical and political tradition [including Ephesians 4:26, "Be angry, but sin not"] suggests that victims of injustice ought not get angry because doing so would be *counterproductive*."[10] She suggests that proponents of rational politics wrongly claim that anger is irrational, saying, "Little wonder then that defenders of anger tend to be suspicious of the liberal enchantment with the idea of a rational politics. A rational politics has no room for anger, and so no room for one of the few weapons available to the oppressed."[11] She shows that in the history of philosophy the question of the moral value of anger was only ever "about the powerful: free, wealthy men, with the capacity for unchecked violence. . . . It was simply taken for granted that women and slaves had no business getting angry; the debate about anger was never about them"; so, when an argument claims that there is no rational need for anger, "we neglect, as we have always neglected, those who were never allowed to be angry, the slaves and women who have the power of neither the state nor the sword."[12] If anger is a force that helps people identify violated values and have energy to unite, then white supremacy culture maintains control more easily if brown and Black people's anger is seen as counterproductive or irrational.

Gotham Writers Workshop faculty member Rachel Simon and activist and speaker Valerie Kaur have to directly coach their hearers that anger is a right response to injury. Simon writes:

> Asian American Girls . . . you have a right to feel angry. . . . Time and time again, Asian American experiences and voices have been diminished and ignored. Asian American elders and children have been horrifically harassed and attacked for years. . . . But to acknowledge this racism is seen as wrong in the eyes of so many. . . . When we experience racism, we learn to quietly smile and move on. . . . When we are angry, though, we make noise and make space—in other words, we challenge the white patriarchy that tells us that we are too insignificant to pay attention to because of our race and our gender.[13]

Kaur unswervingly endorses praiseworthy anger:

> I thought of all of us who have been trained to suppress our rage—women, especially women of color. Rage is a healthy, normal, and necessary response to trauma. It is a rightful response to the social traumas of patriarchy, white supremacy, misogyny, homophobia, transphobia, and poverty. But we live in a culture that punishes us when we show our teeth—we are called hysterical when we raise our voice; we are less likely to be believed when we tell our story with fury; and, if we are anything other than deferential with an officer, we might get

hurt or shot, and even then, our deference might not make a difference. Black and brown people have been schooled in the suppression of our emotions as a matter of survival.[14]

For Kaur it's personal. As a Sikh American raising a wonderful child, she reflects on mothering: "There will be moments when I cannot protect [my son] when he is seen as a terrorist, just as black people in America are still seen as criminal; brown people, illegal; Queer and Trans people, immoral; indigenous people, savage; women and girls as property. And when they fail to see our bodies as some mothers' child, it becomes easier to ban us, detain us, deport us, imprison us, sacrifice us for the illusion of security."[15] These insults are meant to keep people docile and easy to control, which assists whiteness in reigning supreme.

Another tactic to minimize people's agency is to make "angry" a name-calling label. In her potent autobiography, *Eloquent Rage*, professor of women's and gender studies and Africana studies Brittany Cooper shows that people's anger—especially Black people's anger—can be used by society to reduce them. She notes, "Angry Black Women get dismissed all the time . . . The story goes that Angry Black Women scare babies, old people, and grown men. This is absurd. And it is a lie."[16]

Once anger is culturally unacceptable (at least for certain people), white supremacy culture gains another layer of protection from challenges to its rule. Cultural control is craftily exerted to make it harder for groups to acknowledge injustices and sustain energy to oppose them. Through complex, albeit repressive, cultural construction, society has arrived at a place where the group who can most acceptably express anger in public are white males, and the people most shunned when expressing public anger are those who inhabit multiple intersectional realities. Today, the culturally dominant can express anger and gain more authority, while anger from those facing structural oppressions can lose authority through transparent public anger.[17] Since anger is a response to injustice, this social arrangement of access to public expression of anger is ludicrously inverted. This upside-down cultural arrangement seems at odds with a virtue ethics aimed at the greatest flourishing possible for the whole population.

Being culturally conditioned not to know how to use one's own anger has hindered people when they were ready to bring about social change. Kaur shares her own story of arrest for protesting and how she discovered her need for anger:

I had always thought that my privilege—citizenship, education, literacy—formed a sort of membrane of protection between me and state violence. But in entering a fight against the state and its foot soldiers, on behalf of brown people, as a brown woman, those privileges thinned to nothingness. The officers who hurt and harassed me operated as arms of the state, and the state was marshaling all its power to suppress dissent. Now the state had my body, which meant that it also had the power to silence my voice and break my skin and justify it. . . . In that moment, curled up on the floor of the cell, I knew that I would need to access something deeper and more fiery in me if I was going to face this kind of Goliath. I just didn't know what it was or how to find it.[18]

Anger is part of the antidote to resignation and part of the loving fire that funds movement on behalf of impoverished and marginalized people in the face of white supremacy and related systemic oppressions.

Many reasons exist to refuse to comply with the suppression of anger, especially where it is tied to cultural production of white superiority. For one, suppression of anger doesn't decrease its presence. P. J. Quartana and John W. Burns, chronic pain researchers in the field of psychology, write, "Attempts to suppress anger may amplify pain sensitivity by ironically augmenting perception of the irritating and frustrating qualities of pain."[19] In other words, repressing anger does not eliminate pain—it increases it. Anger needs to be worked through, not quashed. Second, pressure to mislabel emotions muddles and delays clarity about oppression. Leaning on the experiments of social scientists, Soraya Chemaly shows that diverse women suffer pain, depression, and captivity when society deprives them of acceptable expressions of anger. For example, she cites a 2011 UCLA study showing that while certain men in the United States are allowed to express anger, diverse women are expected to exhibit sadness when responding emotionally to perceived harm. She writes, "When we call our anger sadness instead of anger, we often fail to acknowledge what is wrong, specifically in a way that discourages people from imagining and pursuing change. Sadness, as an emotion, is paired with acceptance. Anger, on the other hand, invokes the possibility of change and fighting back."[20] For Chemaly, women's abilities to communicate emotions and move civil and political spheres to action are crucial. Third, refusing to harness anger undercuts the energy needed to resist injustice and, thereby, benefits the maintenance of oppressive systems. Those in power benefit from masses of people being encultured not to get angry. The culture frustrating people's access to anger or to skillfulness with anger can become an additional part of people's oppression.

Not only does disallowing, mislabeling, or refusing anger fail to dissipate anger, suppressing anger is a misguided goal. Dalit feminist and Hebrew Bible scholar S. Helen Chukka names two harms of anger suppression and two reasons anger expression is needed in marginalized communities:

- Suppression of anger in public spaces transforms into feelings of shame and humiliation and can have ripple effects negatively impacting relationships in domestic spaces.
- Expression of anger in public spaces is often associated with being "uncivilized," especially for individuals from marginal social locations. Some are willing to risk such labels in order to resist and confront dominant forces of power.
- Expression of anger is an affirmation of human dignity.
- Expression of anger builds trust among marginal communities and fosters solidarities.[21]

Those who seek good for marginalized communities need increased familiarity with anger. Cooper calls people to get more in touch with anger for the sake of survival. Cooper invokes rage as a legitimate political emotion for Black and Indigenous Women who have and continue to experience multiple oppressions. By political emotion, she means an emotion able to sway publics in ways that can potentially effect structural change She calls Black Women to the emotion of rage because "focused with precision, it can become a powerful source of energy serving progress and change."[22] Rage, in Cooper's estimation, can both smash things and dismantle systems and be productive and constructive. Cooper focuses on building spaces and systems that center and benefit, politically and structurally, Black Women and Girls. Cooper calls for tearing down harmful structures and building back prosocial ones.

While Cooper puts a call out for a dismantling and rebuilding, philosopher Myisha Cherry shows that anger is necessary to identify abuse, to communicate love, and to form community. For Myisha Cherry, Black rage is explicitly not excessive or violent. No. She says, "Note that Black rage's usefulness does not depend on its ability to bring about any reform. Black rage (with its love, criticality, and creativeness) is useful because it communicates disapprobation of injustice and affirms love and value of and solidarity with Blacks."[23] People's anger doesn't have to be productive for the dominant culture in order to be good, but it does show what people love and to whom they are connected.

ANGER IN THE CHURCH

Anger has both shown up and been shut down in the church. Interestingly, Scripture's interpretation and prevalence of godly anger has not been proportionally echoed in traditional church teachings, which have more often resorted to Stoic philosophy's negative interpretation of anger. Stoic philosophy's outsized hermeneutic advantage in the church needs to be questioned in favor of the Bible's own more positive and nuanced view.

Stoic philosophy's negative view of anger has been incorporated into US theology to such an extent that it has muted the diverse and nuanced perspective presented in the Bible. It is Stoic philosophers, not biblical authors, who consistently view anger as only morally problematic. Seneca—a Stoic from ancient Rome—defined anger as a "desire to inflict punishment"[24] and thought of it as a form of being out of control. He taught that anger was irrational and did not have a place in the good life. This Stoic view is alive in congregations and mislabeled as a theological or religious view when it is, in fact, only one philosophical viewpoint.

Biblical Accounts of Anger

Beyond Jesus's temple-table-flipping in John 2:13–22, there are biblical accounts of anger that we've been taught not to see.[25] Jesus was angry aplenty and did ministry and healing while angry. Although not in the scope of this book, these include seeing Jesus "moved with anger" (ἐμβριμάομαι (embrimaomai)) in Mark 1:43, Matthew 9:30, and John 11:33, as well as references to Jesus's affect in Matthew 6:5–18, Mark 12:38–44, and Matthew 23. Three other stories are worth exploring here. These are the New Testament stories of Jesus healing a man with a shriveled hand, Jesus healing a woman crippled for eighteen years, and little children coming to Jesus.

In Mark 3:2–6, Jesus shows up at synagogue at the same time as a man with a withered hand. Some Pharisees "were watching him to see whether he would cure him on the Sabbath, so that they might accuse him" (Mark 3:2). Jesus invites the man forward and asks the Pharisees what is lawful—doing good or harm on the Sabbath. When they remain silent, Jesus "looked around at them with anger; he was grieved at their hardness of heart and said to the man, 'Stretch out your hand.'" Pharisees were using the letter of the law to subvert the good of the law, and Jesus defied both their stinginess and their misinterpreted rules.

In yet another confrontation with church leaders in Luke 13:10–17, Jesus was angry when he refutes the leader of the synagogue who would keep an ailing woman bent another day. He says, "You hypocrites! Does not each of you on the Sabbath untie his ox or his donkey from the manger and lead it to water?[16] And ought not this woman, a daughter of Abraham whom Satan bound for eighteen long years, be set free from this bondage on the Sabbath day?" (Luke 13:15b–16). His use of the term "hypocrites" shows anger. Jesus is incensed as he points out their double standard.

Both Mark 10:13–16 and Matthew 19:13–15 tell stories of children coming for Jesus's touch of blessing. It appears the disciples were trying to protect Jesus from getting overwhelmed. They spoke sternly, dissuading those approaching Jesus. "But when Jesus saw this, he was indignant and said to them, 'Let the children come to me.'" The word ἀγανακτέω that is translated "indignant" means to be angry, vexed. Children getting turned away from him angered Jesus, who goes on to say that the reign of God belongs to those who can receive it as children.

The kinds of things that anger Jesus include misinterpretation of the law, prioritizing rules over people, and blocking access to those ready to receive God's reign. And when Jesus is angry, he tends to do ministry that specifically includes healing and increasing access for marginalized people to what they need. So, the church, rooted in the narratives of the Bible, has a stockpile of stories and images of Jesus simmering when vulnerable people might be sidelined or harmed. Jesus was energized to draw people into care and to address the structural conditions that kept people down.

The Hebrew Bible also offers many instances of God's anger. The Old Testament regularly presents God's anger as evidence of God's faithfulness to God's people. The Old Testament often describes God with nostrils flaring at injustice. Psalm 18:8 says, "Smoke rose from his nostrils; consuming fire came from his mouth." The Psalmist addresses this in the context of a story about people who are violent against those keeping God's ways, saying "to the faithful you [God] show yourself faithful" (v. 25).

The Hebrew Bible uses the word אַף (*aph*) 166 times to show God's anger. Of these, thirteen acknowledged that God is slow to anger. That leaves 153 times the Hebrew Bible shows that God, although characteristically slow to anger, still got angry. Of those occurrences, thirty-two times God's anger flared when people did not trust God, another sixty-six instances were anger when people followed other gods.

The Hebrew Bible also shows five times when God's anger flared against oppression of the marginalized. For example, in Exodus 22:21–24, God says, "You shall not wrong or oppress a resident alien, for you were aliens in the land of Egypt.[22] You shall not abuse any widow or orphan.[23] If you do abuse them, when they cry out to me, I will surely heed their cry;[24] my אַף (aph) will burn." God values the well-being of the vulnerable. When that well-being is violated, God is in touch with anger such that God moves to "heed their cry"—to address the cause of suffering and restore flourishing lives.

Churches and the Suppression of Anger

Despite abundant biblical references to God's and Jesus's anger, Christianity has gotten used by empire to culturally suppress anger. Concepts like the seven deadly sins, certain interpretations of biblical texts, and denominational teachings alike have taught church folx to think of anger as wrong and its use as morally problematic. In the fourth century, monk Evagrius Ponticus included anger when he penned what he called the eight evil thoughts.[26] Two centuries later, St. Gregory the Great reworked the list in his *Commentary on the Book of Job*. He took pride off the list, naming it as the driver of the seven deadly sins. Through the intervening centuries and up to the present, wrath or anger has remained on the list. Christians have tacitly thought of anger as a sin and have preached that way about it. For example, Martin Luther was known at table and from pulpit to caution against "envy, wrath, avarice, and disbelief."[27]

Denominational teachings have reinforced negative views of anger. In the Roman Catholic Church, Jerome, a purportedly angry saint, got canonized, but anger is usually cited as a mark against him. Womanist ethicist and theological educator Selina Rachel Stone notes that Pentecostalism tends to suspect that emotions tempt people to sin. "Anger then, is not associated with holiness for human beings, even though the 'wrath of God' is considered valid and acceptable in theological terms."[28]

Although the church has participated in anger suppression in Christians' lives, the church actually needs anger in order to be the Church. Episcopal priest Kira Austin-Young, writing about Mark 9:38–50, which reproves anyone who trips up a young person, says that "in a world where war rages, where racism and gender inequality run amok, where economic inequality is only growing, where our leaders work to divide and not unite us, Christians should stand with the anger of the vulnerable, of the little ones, of those who are most affected by injustice in the world. As women, if we are paying attention at all, we should be mad."[29]

WOMEN AND GENDER-DIVERSE PEOPLE

Little research is available about gender-diverse people's experience of anger. A 2023 psychological study asked how gender shapes anger and aggression.[30] Given the dearth of research, discussing some of the study's results is worthwhile even though two methodological problems in this study need to be briefly noted. First, by pursuing the connection between anger and aggression from the DSM-5 framework of diagnosis of mental illness, the study problematically conflates anger with aggression and tacitly assesses anger as an illness. Second, this research fitted people's gender into five pre-defined categories. While it is an improvement to move beyond two binaries of women and men, it remains underwhelming because it precludes people from accurately naming their own gender.

Nevertheless, several findings from this study are helpful. The traditionally masculine participants reported the shortest duration of anger, meaning women and people who are gender diverse experienced longer durations of anger. In addition, those who identified with either traditionally masculine or feminine categories—who the authors hypothesized could have bought into and benefitted more from societal norms—reported less anger than people who resisted some cultural norms (e.g., not conforming to gender binaries). The authors hypothesized that people who had already come to resist some norms may also be willing to report more honestly about anger—an emotion that can be considered to have low social desirability. In this study, people who identified as gender fluid and women reported the highest feelings of anger. Questions remain whether gender-nonconforming people experience more anger or are more honestly in touch with their anger.

Even though traditionally masculine people did not *feel* the most anger, they did *express* the most; they "were more likely to engage in anger responses aimed at retribution toward the offender."[31] The amount of anger people feel is not necessarily correlated to the amount of anger people express. What effects does not getting to express anger at a rate equitable to their peers have on people? Families and societies teach rather effectively (and often nonverbally and at young ages) that anger works for some people while it sets others even further back. For centuries, angry displays by people who inhabit dominant social locations increases their authority and ascribed competence. Conversely, anger displayed by people society marginalizes results in less influence and a lower estimation of aptitude. This is not the fault of marginalized people; rather, society has a problem. This problem needs to be exposed because people society marginalizes need access to anger in order to flourish and transform harmful systems.

Women's, gender, and sexuality studies professor Hilary Malatino studies trans people's anger and says that "[anger] is integral to trans survival and flourishing."[32] Anger as a response to unlivable situations helps trans people to move away from toxic relationships and find life-giving community. Naming anger and even amplifying anger can be life preserving and serve trans flourishing. Malatino adds that support is needed in the aftermath of opening oneself to the uses and (internal) impacts of anger. Support after feeling or displaying anger can help people assess the value of that anger and imagine how they would like to craft anger the next time it arises or is called for.

Another study suggested that *experiences* of anger across genders is more consistent than anger *expression*.[33] The research showed that people of all genders share similarities in how they experience anger—what anger feels like, what slights instigate anger, and so on. However, cis males express that anger more readily and publicly than people of other genders. Perhaps the ability to readily discharge one's anger without incurring guilt or decreased authority allows males' anger to be short-lived. This relates to a different study that found that males present more stories of anger in everyday life that are short-lived and external. Conversely, women present more stories of anger that have a longer duration, are internally focused, and related to a negative self-evaluation.[34]

LGBTQIA+ people report less depression and anger when living in supportive communities.[35] Yet even then, Queer people face heightened levels of chronic stress and challenges to their identity. Pastoral theologian Brooke Petersen, who studies trauma faced by Queer people when religious communities "preached hate, told them they were disgusting, and that God wanted to punish them for eternity in the fires of hell," found that part of the pain people experience comes because "the ethical system by which they arranged their lives now no longer includes them."[36] Such harmful exclusions break relationships and open Queer people "to the unspoken anger, rage, and sadness at the frequent and long-term betrayals enacted by people and communities they love."[37] External suggestions that one does not belong with one's own ethical worldview or religious community can become an internalized oppression and leave one driftless in relation to one's ethical and religious beliefs.

Anyone forced to live with dysphoria and anxiety likely would experience anger since their values are regularly violated and their protests to these violations quashed. The more society makes it dangerous for people with nondominant identities to express anger about violated values the more that anger may get internalized. Building on the work of Queer, decolonial, and feminist scholars, professor of philosophy Jen McWeeny exposes "the dominator's view of our angers, which sees them as irrational, unjustified, hypersensitive, and morally and epistemologically unproductive."[38] The dominant culture's dismissal of the anger of BIPOC and gender-diverse people can be a form of gaslighting. McWeeny encourages the embrace of anger responses to structural oppressions. Those working for virtuous social transformation, as well as people living under oppression, have had to come to terms with the fact that those in power benefit from masses of people being enculturated not to get angry.[39] People must get innovative in order to confront culturally constructed, limiting views of anger.

WOMEN'S EXPERIENCES

Women experience anger in many varied ways. Yet, stories of their shared experience of facing US cultural conditioning does reveal some recognizable patterns. Many women can identify with expectations not to have or express anger and personalized diminishment when they do express anger. These challenges make it harder for the world to hear and receive women's anger appropriately—by addressing things that violate women and their values. Since many people are undermotivated to interpret women's anger accurately, women end up laboring more so their anger can land effectively.

Gretchen Clayton, who apprenticed with Kelly, had been "kindly invited" to give up anger as a child. She leans back in her chair saying, "With my Midwest background, anger has always had negative connotations. My family—we don't talk about feelings. It's just 'Everything's good.' We're very nonconfrontational, and so addressing a problem would be a very tense situation. Scary.

Anger is something that we need to just pretend we don't have. Talking with my mom about anger, she was like, 'You can just say "passion." Don't say anger. *"Passion"* might be a better word.'" But Gretchen says, "No, it's anger! You know, I can be angry and still be a lady!"

Sue, herself, was enculturated not to experience or express anger. "I'm one of those people who part of my oppression is you don't get angry—you don't express anger—you probably shouldn't even feel it." She saw a double standard growing up. "It seems it was okay for the man of the house to show anger, but for the women in the family, it wasn't an acceptable expression."

Leaders of the VIA teams with which Kelly worked gathered around a long wooden table in a parish hall and took up a conversation regarding women and anger. Megha Hammaker learned as a young person that "women were not supposed to be angry. Little girls were not supposed to be angry. So, I grew up believing that my anger was wrong. I think there was a core part of me that knew some of it was okay."

Around the table these leaders recognize that their anger had been diminished in many ways: as "noise," as "on your period," as "not relevant." They realize that while trying to communicate rational anger they had been talked over, interrupted, affirmed only in secret, and dismissed: "I thought you were joking!" Women find that their anger is often dismissed as a joke. Soraya Chemaly's research showed, "If you ask women what they fear the most in response to their anger, they don't say 'violence'; they say 'mockery.'"[40]

Kelly traveled with a group of mostly women to the state house in Juneau, Alaska, to meet with some legislators because Alaska still had not accepted Medicaid expansion. This indecision had wreaked havoc inequitably on vulnerable populations in their community.

Kelly recalls a poignant phrase from a legislator who mocked in singsongy tones, "Oh, the little church ladies! They didn't come bringing cookies; they came here with petitions!" Hearing the story, Gretchen quips, "Like you can't be taken seriously!" Kelly adds her interpretation, "Yea. 'You're church ladies; go make us a quilt. Make us a casserole; bake some cookies; do some charity.'"

Although Kelly's group had done their research, planned their strategy, and traveled across the state, still they were diminished by public representatives, who seemed to prefer service and sweets over citizens engaged in public policy.

Jenny Michaelson, a VIA leader, says, "If a woman wants to be effective, she will show her anger in a certain way because it's only tolerated in a certain way. Certainly, we can all be angry, but if I want to do something effective with that anger . . . I just have to handle it better [than men] in order to get what I want out of that. People are uncomfortable with anger. I think that men are uncomfortable with women's anger."

Women face cultural roadblocks to exhibiting anger that looks and sounds angry, so many people develop alternative ways of displaying anger. Some women interviewed noted that their anger tended to come out as tears. Researchers in social and behavioral sciences Agneta Fischer and Catharine Evers found that "women more often report to cry when angry compared to men."[41] The culturally conditioned response of tears can feel invalidating because it gets perceived by others as sadness or being "emotional," which can add an extra layer of anger for those habituated to present in this way.

Expert on women's anger Soraya Chemaly reports that,

> most women asked about anger describe expressing their anger either as sadness or fear. How many people here have cried when they're angry? I really do believe most men would be shocked if they understood how insanely angry women are when they cry. Because crying confirms feminine ideals. It's less threatening. And it's not that we think, "I'm really angry. I should cry now." It's more that we've just been socialized to process this emotion that way, and actually not name it as anger. I, for example, have cried, and then hours, days, weeks, years later come to the realization that I was so pissed off that I could not get words out.[42]

Women are often culturally conditioned not to express anger angrily but to express anger the way they express retreat emotions like fear and sadness. So thorough is this conditioning that women's enculturation to express sadness or fear masks women's anger not only from publics but makes it hard for the women themselves to recognize their own anger. It is problematic that women are conditioned to change their anger and themselves to be socially acceptable when, to a large extent, it is society that needs changing in order to stop injuring women and thereby provoking their anger.

Pamela Twiss, an organizer with National People's Action, and Sue Engh were not in Alaska with the VIA leaders; yet, from their positions in Minnesota, they share related perspectives. Pamela says, "I feel like until I met agitational organizing, I suffered in silence. I was still angry, but I didn't talk about it, I didn't think it was okay to express. I was 'too intense.' And when I first started organizing in this model, I cried all the time. Yes, that was my reaction to being angry when I was expressing it in public." Tears while training tapered and eventually stopped for Pamela but only after some years of coming to terms with her body's manifestation of anger.

Sue realized she not only *expressed* anger in an alternate form, but actually came to *feel alternate emotions* when anger was the root emotion. "So, I think I learned to feel something different when anger might be the real emotion I was experiencing. I might feel frightened, or sad, often expressed in tears and meekness." Enculturation taught Sue to mislabel her anger as fear or sadness and express it in ways that offered public, visual signals (tears, meekness) of a retreat emotion instead of anger. Sometimes people *express* anger in ways that look like sadness; other times people do not even let themselves experience anger and instead *experience* sadness or fear.

Sue, Pamela, and Soraya, taking a close look at anger and expression, find tears to be an expression of anger—albeit an expression masked by cultural conventions of social respectability. Interpreting tears as a potential signal of the presence of anger is beneficial because it enables one to accurately perceive and name a feeling. Although identifying this expression was illuminating, none of these women articulated tears as their preferred or most powerful expression of anger. Tears could helpfully alert them to the violation of some value, but they sought to cultivate other public expressions of anger.

Women have long been shaping their anger so that it comes out looking like sadness or fear—a shaping born from the pressure of iteration after iteration of social conditioning. Shaping anger into a retreat emotion such as sadness or fear is not only inauthentic but also leaves one stuck in that feeling (instead of fueled with anger's energy to act). Fear and sadness are emotions that have historically decreased the power women have to be taken seriously in public spaces. People who shape anger to look like sadness or fear end up with more work to do because they both have to recognize something as anger that is disguised, and they have to resist the retreat emotion and rediscover the approach power of anger that can help them deal with the underlying injustice.

There is a bit of good news for people who already are experienced at shaping anger as fear or sadness, because choreographing anger is not itself an entirely new skill. Instead of shaping anger in ways that may make society feel at ease but unsettle and constrain women, the organizers suggest freeing women to focus their anger in ways that make unjust systems squirm. Women's therapy expert Miriam Greenspan interprets "the underground anger of women as a potential mobilizing force for personal and social change," and says that "typical female 'symptoms' of oppression such as depression, repressed anger, low self-esteem . . . could be re-interpreted as seeds of strength."[43] Women's anger, released from underground and repressed modes, is a powerful force for prosocial change.

Early in her organizing career, Mary embraced potency in how she embodies rising anger. Mary learned to cognitively process what she saw as unjust or inaccurate and to appropriately link the infraction to the offending party. "I will never forget. One day a guy said to me, 'You're just a power-hungry bitch.' And he said it to me at a national training; I think I was in my 3rd year of training. I almost died." She thought, "He's just trying to eliminate me from the conversation by adding 'power-hungry bitch' to it. What he really means is he's threatened by my power. I looked at him and I said, 'I didn't realize you were so perceptive; thank you very much for that compliment.'"

PART II

Foundations of Agapic Anger

To the list of the multiple species of anger already identified, another type is added in this section. It is a form that rises to prominence in the community organizers' stories. Building on the definition of anger as a response to an unjust harm, agapic anger translates harm to a communal level by examining its systemic causes and finding energy to confront and take steps toward structural transformation.

In chapter 5, agapic anger is portrayed as an anger that has cooled sufficiently to be put to good use. It is an anger that can creatively advance genuine human happiness, but it needs to be cultivated in community. This chapter describes agapic anger as comprised of love, hope, and courage. It addresses why it is worth thinking about this difficult emotion and shows how choreography can help develop good anger.

Chapter 6 introduces a sort of dance that transforms existing anger into agapic anger so that it catalyzes communities' flourishing. The chapter concludes by unpacking how anger can move in two directions at once. The women's stories show that good anger is generally characterized by experiences of being repulsed by abusive systems as well as desiring and being motivated to seek social transformation.

Chapter 4 tells Drea's story that highlights rightful anger that is present when life accumulates multiple injustices, and shows how, even amid wrongs, that anger can be put to good use. She didn't get a zero-entry glide in or out of her childhood, though she does provide a gentle, secure life for her own daughter. Drea had to wade in depths from the start. Her story tells how she turned some of her anger into confidence. She wasn't going to let people stereotype her as angry and sideline her. So she used her anger to do strategic steps: Plan. "Roll up your sleeves. Pop your collar. Get to work." Her story shows that good anger probably looks like confidence on most people.

CHAPTER FOUR

Pop Your Collar and Dig In
Meet Drea Hall

Andrea "Drea" Hall walks into a room, and you can feel she has brought along something intangible but very present. Her confidence takes up residence along with all the other participants, and she uses it to really see people—both those whose status takes up the most space and those whose life circumstances have diminished their position. Her confidence also lets her see calmly behind any given situation. Her hand is not forced. She determines what action her institution will take.

"So I'm originally from Oshkosh, Wisconsin. My mom is from Jamaica; and she went to school in Oshkosh—that's how we got there. My family: they were educated. My mom went to college there [in Oshkosh], and her brother went on to be a chemist. So, I see an education always at the forefront as a goal of mine because my family had attained it.

"It's just my mother suffered from mental and physical illnesses that got in the way of her sustaining work." For parts of her young life, Drea's "mom had public housing [or] some type of affordable housing." Drea also "experienced homelessness as young as five and as old as twenty. So I lived in a couple of shelters. At one point, my mom was in a relationship with someone who I would consider the abuser. We would stay with him; go to the shelter; stay with him. So eventually the last time I lived in a shelter I was fifteen years old. It was a domestic violence shelter, so that was another layer of trauma that I had to deal with, and I definitely was angry. I said, 'I'm not going back to stay with him.' I never went back to live with the abuser. Instead, I went with my friend, and then eventually my mom was able to get some type of funding, and she was able to get an apartment again.

"I was an angry teenager growing up. My anger was probably towards my mother and towards the men that she chose over me. I probably was angry about my friends' parents who judged me. They thought I would end up like my mother, or they didn't encourage their children to be with me because they thought I grew up on the wrong side of the train track. I was angry at the police who would racial profile us for being Black walking down the street or driving. . . . They definitely didn't believe in [me, and thought] I would have no future. When I was a teenager, I definitely saw the difference" in how police treated people of different races.

"My friends would tell me" things that happened. "I have white friends; I have Black friends and more. When I would be with my white friends, you probably wouldn't get approached by the police if we're walking down the street, right? If we're in a store in the mall, sometimes we did, and then my friends will be, 'Well, that's weird. Police never have done that before.' And then they realize it's because *I'm* with them. And they're like, 'Huh! Interesting.' Or when I was with my all-Black friends if a police vehicle goes by, it's highly likely that he's gonna *talk* to us. That's like, 'Why are you talking to us, you know? Are you worried [for] us? Probably not. It's the middle of the day, you know. You're just wondering if we're up to no good.' And that, to me, is profiling. That's what they do. And yes, [I've got] a lot of stories of racial profiling and feeling harassed by it.

"In Oshkosh I was the only African American to graduate out of my high school in 1999. I wasn't the only one that was there; I was the only one that made it. We all could have made it if people would've invested. My own guidance counselor was surprised that I was going to go to college. When I went to go fill out applications to go to college,

he said, 'Oh, you're going to college?'
And I said, 'Oh, yeah, just like Sally and Ricky, you know, like everyone else . . .'
And he's like, 'Oh, well, I thought you were going to go into the working world.'
And I'm like, 'Hmm, okay.'

And that for me was another ball of anger. For me it was an anger that was like, 'I'm gonna prove them all wrong.' I felt the injustice—I probably didn't call it that—I just called it wrong or racist. It came down to how I was treated and the injustice I experienced.

"To me, going to college broke that cycle of poverty and homelessness and, to a certain extent, my anger. When I went to college, I wasn't the only Black person anymore. I actually got some of the best grades: I got a 4 point my first semester in school, never dropped below 3.3, traveled the world, became a McNair Scholar.[1] And as I did all those things, my anger definitely died down because I'm like, 'Oh, people *do* believe in me,' or, 'I am able to do these opportunities that my colleagues who have money got to do while I was growing up; now I get to do them in in college.'"

Drea noticed that sometimes her anger limited her or got used against her. "My [extended] family thought I was angry. I don't think they understood that I had been homeless, that my mom was not consistent or stable, so they just looked at me as angry until they started hearing more about what I had been through. And they're like, 'Oh, no wonder you might be angry,' and, 'Our bad; we weren't there for you.'

"It was the end of my freshman year of college. I finished my first year up great—great grades. I didn't have any place to go because my mom lost her apartment again, and so I had to live with my uncle. I think he definitely judged me. He had two girls, and I felt like he was trying to protect his girls a little. So he had his picture of me being angry, and eventually he said, 'Oh, well, I don't think you can stay here.' I'm like, 'Oh, okay, that was my summer plan. Well, what am I gonna do?' And then I asked the other uncle in Jersey, and he said, 'The apple doesn't fall too far from the tree.' That's a quote that I have, and that I hold on to because, if anything, it gave me motivation to prove them all wrong. I think I was angry, and I saw how people reacted towards me when I was angry, and I didn't get what I wanted per se. I probably got judged or sidelined. So instead, I said, 'You know what, I'm going to be great at school; I'm going to find friends and relationships that support me and lift me up; I'm gonna sign up for any program at school that will help me be a better student and get me where I need to go.' And I just started planning.

"I was like, 'You know what? I'm tired of being angry.' I think that these people judge me, and the only thing I can do is prove them wrong, and that goes with actions. For example, I didn't have a driver's license when I was twenty years old. I got a full-time job working in a factory at twenty years old, doing things twenty-year-olds don't want to do, but I did it so I could get my license, go back to school as a sophomore with a car. . . . And so I think it's just flipping the script from like, 'Oh, I'm angry, and F these people' to 'I'm gonna let this motivate me to do better. I'm going to prove them wrong.'

"And proving them wrong would make me happy. For example, remember the guidance counselor who thought I was not going to college. Yeah, I got a 4 point on my first semester. I got a card that says, 'African American highest GPA Award.' I went back to my school, and I took my plaque. 'Oh, hey! Mr. So and so, you remember me?'

And he's like, "Oh, yeah."
Holding out my award, I said, "Yeah, I'm at Whitewater."
And he's like, "Oh, wow! My goodness."
I said, "Yeah, if I would've listened to you, I wouldn't have gone to college. You could have made me feel lesser or made me question my ability, but, instead, I thought you were being discriminative."

A young person is not supposed to have to deal with the intersectional traumas and resultant angers she had experienced. Drea recognizes that and says, "Trauma has impacted me. I didn't meet my father till I was thirty-nine. So a young girl without a father—that can be detrimental or impact your relationship with other men. I definitely think that the lack of healthy relationships impacted myself. And further, the trauma I felt around abandonment: you know, my mom did the best she could, but there were a lot of things I missed out on. I took my trauma, and I learned from it. I'm learning how to raise a daughter without exposing her to trauma or to intentional experiences of trauma. I try to make her life be as a kid. You know, at her age or a little older I knew what rent was and that we were behind on rent. My daughter doesn't know anything about that. If anything, she knows the difference between being a homeowner and a renter now because she watched me buy my first home last year.

"I actually went to therapy when I was twenty-seven—that's when I first moved to Chicago." Drea smiles to herself as she recalls, "And I had this therapist [who] said, 'You have this complex—and she's angry. And she's called Xena: Warrior Princess. Xena comes out to protect you. She was there probably for when you felt abandoned or you felt you just need to be protected. She was there in a way to defend you—to defend yourself. And now that you're older, Drea, you don't need Xena.'

I'm like, "Oh," [and nods in reflection].
She's like, "You're not about to be homeless. You're not having to depend on your mom anymore. You're an adult living your life. You don't need [Xena]. You don't need the anger."
And I'm like, "Oh, okay."
"And if anything, the anger can be, you know, put towards other things. But it doesn't have to be in your life because you don't have those experiences anymore."
I'm like, "Oh, wow." So that was kind of cool to hear.

Drea notices that anger can be put toward "the organizing and the work. So there might be something like my last position—I was working in juvenile justice, and I could be angry about how the police are treating the youth or keeping the youth in adult jails for long periods of time. Instead of calling someone up and being angry, I help people pivot. 'No, let's write a letter. Let's write a policy. Let's tell the governor.' You know, there are solutions that you can do that are strategic, methods that you can implement that won't make you look like the angry Black woman."

There are forms of anger that Drea doesn't want her daughter to have to hold. "I don't want her to have anger towards [issues of] her well-being. Like my anger was, 'Oh, I have no food. Why?' 'Oh, I can't go to volleyball camp when I'm one of the best players on the team because I don't have money.' Yeah, I don't want her to experience any economic anger. There'll be times where I tell her, 'No, you're not getting that video game; you're not getting those roller skates, or whatever.'

"But I think I tell her and show her there is healthy anger. I mean, the work we do—she was in a picket with a sign that says, 'We demand . . .' when she was like five years old. So I think she sees my friends—they're a congresswoman, they're an alderman, they are all sorts of people, and we're all agitated about something. We're willing to do something about it. And that's what I want to show her: it's one thing to be angry and just sit there and be angry or take it out on people. It's another thing to turn it into some type of solution, which would address your anger hopefully.

My daughter told me, "Mommy, you know what I love the most about
you?"
I said, "What?"
She said, "Your confidence."
And I'm like, "Ah, [nodding] confidence. Hmm."

"And that is exactly what I have. I think my anger lifted up my confidence.
I turned some of the anger into confidence. Anger can make you feel sad,
doubtful, insecure. But for me, I'm like, 'Oh, I'm angry, and I'm gonna do
something about it. Yeah. Watch out. Roll up your sleeves. Pop your collar.
Get to work.'"

THE SYSTEM CAN LET YOU DOWN

"For me, I guess what led me to social work and justice work is experiencing
injustice and anger at a young age. When it comes to the profession, I thought
I wanted to be a social worker—like a straight up DCSF [Department for
Children, Schools and Families] social worker—taking parents' children—you
know parents that weren't responsible—because I thought maybe I should
have been taken but I wasn't taken.

"I felt, as time went on, that I had a duty to succeed: my family came here
for a reason, and I can't keep on this cycle of poverty and homelessness. And
so I said, 'You know, I'll do social work.' But then I got exposed to social
work's direct service—like in shelters and different things—and I would be
so very emotional. I would cry with them. I would try to talk with them. I
probably enabled more than I empowered, and that's not a good thing in social
work. I think the poverty I experienced myself and the anger I had growing
up [came alongside] as I got older, and I realized, 'I think I'm best suited for
macro-level social work.' And that's what got me involved in community
organizing."

From the University of Wisconsin-Whitewater, Drea went to grad school
at Washington University in St. Louis, where she encountered and was drawn
to the macro level of social work. Then she got recruited to Chicago in 2005
by Service Employee International Union (SEIU), one of the largest unions
in the country. SEIU grounded her in organizing's tactics, strategies, and
agitation skills.

"Then I left for the Chicago Coalition for the Homeless," which organizes "to prevent and end homelessness because we believe housing is a human right in a just society,"[2] and where she was a senior organizer. "And that's when I again [was] introduced to my life stories, and I shared those stories and experiences with other homeless folks, or youth, or funders, or judges." From there, I "went to Chicago Public Schools, where I worked with parent engagement" as a senior family and community engagement manager. "So I was, if anything, trying to agitate parents around them caring for their child's education to the point that they do something about it: Go run for LSC [Local School Council, an elected body involved in school decision making]. Go be on the PAC [Parent Action Council]. If there's opportunity to talk with the principal, then go talk with the principal." Next, Drea worked with the Illinois Department of Human Services as the director of strategy, equity, and transformation until she moved into the position of executive director of the Illinois Juvenile Justice Commission.

Drea is now the CEO of MYSI Corporation. MYSI is explicit that religious values inform their work of providing temporary housing and community-based support for those experiencing housing insecurity. In their press release, MYSI wrote, "With over 18 years of experience in serving Chicago families, [Drea] has advocated for affordable housing, passed legislation and policies to reform the criminal justice system, worked with students and families to increase parent engagement, mobilized faith-based institutions, and collaborated with national partners to address racial inequities in the juvenile justice system."[3] Drea's career choices have consistently put her in the position of serving youth put at risk by things beyond their control and accompanying families who need secure housing. She's been able and willing to channel her anger at what she had to endure into leveraging improved systems for today's youth.

"I think I teach people that it's okay to be angry. Like the youth I work with right now—I work with DCSF Youth ([ages] 14 to 21, mainly 17 to 21), and they're angry. They're very angry because they feel the system let them down. Their parents let them down. Their future is uncertain. And so I say, 'You know, it's okay to be angry, but you have to also pivot that anger to strategize, to create hope in your life. You can be angry, and you can even live in it for a [bit], but you can't live in it forever. You gotta step out of it. And what can we do to help you step out of it?' So we provide tools to help them manage their anger."

CHURCH: A PLACE OF HOPE, PLACE OF GRATITUDE

"I feel like I personally didn't come into Christ until I was in my thirties. My mom grew up Catholic, and when she came to the United States, I think she gravitated towards Christian[ity] in general. She tried to get us involved, but lack of transportation and inconsistency [kept us from getting there]. I never really experienced church growing up.

"It wasn't until I had my daughter at thirty-four, I said, 'I think I need more than just me and her. I think I need a village, a team. When I look around at some of my friends who are faithful people, their church is a backbone for them. The church is like a safe place for them and to a certain extent like a second family.' So I started researching churches. By 2014 I found Soul City Church. So I've been going to Soul City Church—it's nondenominational but very much feels like the evangelical church, and it's in the West Loop area in Chicago. I got baptized there in 2017. And just been going there since.

"My church is used to newcomers. So I went through a couple of different kind of trainings or Bible series. So for me it's learning. It's teaching my daughter from two years old what it means to go to church, which I didn't have. I like my church because they do believe in justice. My pastor listened when I said, 'Hey, this is what my nonprofit does. They work with churches to move us from mercy and charity to justice. Jesus was the first organizer. You know, that's how we kind of look at it as organizers who believe in Christ.'

There have been plenty of ways Drea heard religious people discourage anger. "When I think about religion, what comes to mind is, 'Don't show your feelings of anger; you're supposed to be a good Christian, right? We're supposed to live in the life of Jesus.' And they'll reference a Bible story that shows anger and what happened from that anger [to show that anger goes awry]. Therefore, I don't think the Bible necessarily thinks anger is a good thing. It's obviously a feeling that you have, but you need to figure out how to manage it."

But there's another reality, too. "I think some stories of Jesus [show anger as beneficial]. He guided people towards fighting for what they believe in. He might not have called it anger, or maybe he did—like turn that anger into. . . . But he touched people that might experience trauma and tragedy, and he said, 'You can take that and use it towards good.' I don't think [church leaders] ever said, 'Don't be angry,' when they talked about Jesus. I think it also was like a factor in empowering people to be better."

"In the beginning of me going to church, I was probably angrier or sadder about my life. I think church helped me be more grateful. Instead of being angry and sad, church helped me kind of flip it to be more hopeful and grateful."

CHAPTER FIVE

Making Anger Good

Elements and Movements of Agapic Anger

Transformative agapic anger is formed through interanimated movements of love, hope, and courage. In addition, there are three more prominent characteristics of agapic anger. Agapic anger is a cooled anger, contributes to people's happiness, and needs to be practiced in community. Finally, it is important to be honest about detriments of anger; four specific areas of caution are explored.

LOVE MAKES ANGER GOOD

Good anger works for love. It is in the service of love—especially the love of justice. Such love predisposes people to affirm the common good and seek social structures that promote it. Love-based anger is characterized by hope and courage.

A virtue ethics of emotion distinguishes among kinds of love. Of particular note are *amor* and *caritas*. *Amor* as an emotion is a feeling that tends toward what a person perceives to be suitable and pleasant for herself or for others she includes in her circle of concern. The feeling *amor* differs neighbor to neighbor depending on a sense of connection. *Caritas*, on the other hand, is a virtue of the will— where virtue is a habit formed over time by making right judgments time and time again. *Caritas* is not a feeling but a habit that consistently impacts how a person orients herself toward what she judges to be good or lacking in goodness.

A love of justice is rooted in *caritas* and forms people's dispositions to be oriented rightly toward the common good. In the field of virtue ethics, justice refers to a virtue that is specifically oriented toward action for the benefit of others and for the sake of what is truly good. Ethicist Jean Porter says practicing justice gives an "enduring orientation toward the common good to the agent's judgements, feelings, and actions."[1] It is not a feeling but a habit that spreads its impact across a person's dispositions, desires, and decisions. Aquinas praises justice as foremost among moral virtues because it tends toward the good of other people and not only the good of the virtuous person herself.[2]

Should the pursuit of increased justice become arduous or the achievement of greater justice uncertain, a person oriented toward justice tends to experience anger. Professor of philosophy Paul Woodruff writes, "Our capacity for anger functions as our sensitivity to injustice. Anger and justice are yoked. An individual is just insofar as his or her anger is keyed to injustice. . . . Learning to be angry better is part of acquiring justice."[3] In Gretchen's religious worldview, for example, people are understandably incensed when a neighbor or group of neighbors suffer injustice at the hands of yet other neighbors, be they individuals or institutions. On Aquinas's view, too, anger at its best is rooted in a love of justice.

Anger, in turn, is predicated on hope. In order to define hope, Aquinas notes several conditions. First, hope faces toward the good it wants, which distinguishes hope from fear (which regards what it dreads and wants to get away from); second, hope is future-oriented, not focused on that which is present and already possessed but on that which is future and not yet in hand; and, third, the goal of hope is something that is difficult yet possible to obtain.[4] Hope can be thought of as a desire for a particular good to be realized in the future—a good that will likely be difficult but possible to attain. Anger is oriented toward overcoming an injustice a person deems worth fighting for, and hope provides a future-orientation and a belief that the desired possibility is attainable. Kelly recognizes that hope depends, in some ways, on anger. "At some point you *must* be able to reconcile that you have hope because today you are angry—or today in some way you are not satisfied. And if you can mobilize around that dissatisfaction or that anger, then that's actually what gives us the hope." Hope is a crucial component of the women's anger as they address obstacles. Their ability to envision a different future and to discern what they need to get there was born of hope. Hope continues to feed a journey and strengthen resolve so people and communities can continue to move toward the good they love even when they face setbacks.

There is a point of tension when hope imagines the desired good one has in mind, but an unavoidable obstacle is threatening the path forward. Hope can show the good beyond the barrier. When the barrier is a wrong that has already occurred, then a force is needed to move through the obstacle. Anger is one energizing force that can catalyze movement through an obstacle. Anger adds its own oomph to hope when a person can neither accept nor go around an obstacle and knows that she must go through it.

The process of anger is often aided by the virtue of courage. Aquinas quotes Tully to define courage as "deliberate facing of dangers and bearing of toils,"[5] and says that courage occurs only where love and hope are present.[6] Courage is a habit that allows a person not to be overwhelmed by fear. Instead, it permits a person to overcome fear by deliberately forming a disposition to face, bear up under, or surmount harm in pursuit of a desired good. Courage is formed over a long period of time, but it becomes visible when harm threatens a person, and they have what it takes to confront it. Courage is needed to choose to love despite the fact that loving and continuing to hope in the face of obstacles opens a person to pain. Courage is needed to press through an obstacle instead of feeling resignation and despair in the face of what is difficult. Anger can help a brave person to remain firm in attacking an obstacle.[7] Aquinas references Aristotle when he asserts, "Of all the cases in which fortitude arises from a passion, the most natural is when [one] is brave through anger, making [their] choice and acting for a purpose."[8]

Courage is hard-won through repeated tries at feeling, thinking, and acting courageously, but with practice it can become a disposition. Taking a close look at the story of the Syrophoenician woman, Kelly has trainees shout out the many layered ways she defied the cultural expectations of her day in order to confront Jesus for the sake of her daughter's survival. Kelly was taught to keep her head down, but she says, "I defy this each day I go to work. . . . Organizing put me in close proximity to those who were hurting and demanded that I not *help* them but *join* them on their *own* journey." Courage marks the gait of each of these women. Mary encouraged a woman at a training:

> "What kind of female are you to have survived that by yourself without any help? To have escaped and to be sitting in Chicago, Illinois, today?"

And she couldn't help but get a little grin on her face, right? Like "Well, yeah."

I said, "So tell me how the hell did you do it?"

A COOLED ANGER

For agapic anger to be done well, it cannot be hot and fiery. Mary notes that "if it's going to be effective, it has to be cold." A cooled anger is not a cool hatred that wants ill for someone. Rather, this anger is one rooted in love and does not seek payback.

Saul Alinsky, a community organizer with the Chicago-based Industrial Areas Foundation, references a cool anger in his 1969 preface to his 1946 *Reveille for Radicals*. Alinsky reflected on how he had changed in the quarter century between the original book and the subsequent edition. "I have learned to freeze my hot anger into cool anger and to make my intuitive irreverence conscious, to challenge not only the opposition but myself. . . . In short, cool anger and conscious understanding based on experience have made my actions far more calculated, deliberate, directive, and effective."[9]

For Mary, it is simply common sense. "I just think about it. You have got to have some distance. And not necessarily 'cold,' but you have to have some distance between that emotional hotbed—explosive hotbed—so that you can look at it and say, 'I am royally angry about this, and what the heck am I going to do about it?' You can't even think strategically when you are in the middle of that hotbed, right?" An anger that is so much on fire that it cannot be directed by the one who feels it is generally not ready to be expressed. In Mary's experience, the crucial thing about cooled anger is not its coolness per se but its consciousness, endurance, and critical distance.

Sue also contrasts cooled anger with hot anger. "A certain kind of anger is not what I'm looking for—not red-hot rage but cold, hard determination. You *do* have to move from one to the other—they're not two opposites. Hot cools down into cold, which can be strategic, targeted. That's the useful kind." She says that hot anger "can't be sustained—you're not going to stay in that heat. So, if I want to make it useful, I'm going to turn it into something I can manage strategically." A measured use of cooled anger is key to how organizers choreograph anger.

With anger cooled off, people are able to gain the critical distance they need from anger's initial surge in order to carefully come to conclusions and plan best paths forward. When people reflect on their anger, they can deal with their internal resistance to and discomfort with anger, especially if that resistance and discomfort are culturally constructed barriers that silence and subdue people who are socialized to internalize their anger in forms like sadness and depression. Parishioners or leaders ready to invest in their own transformation benefit from a mentor to bring thought to bear on their own anger, to make the energy of anger more intelligible, and to discover anger as a potential source of power.

HAPPY ANGRY PEOPLE

Many in the United States think of angry people as aggressive and impulsive. However, agapic anger that people can harness does not necessarily turn people into angry people. They do not necessarily become aggressive or impulsive. The anger to which the women assent contributes to their *eudaimonia*—that is, it contributes to their happiness and well-being. Kelly says "I don't come across as an angry person." Indeed, Kelly's calm, competent, discerning comportment pairs well with her witty remarks and penchant for storytelling.

Mary, referring to her organizer husband, expresses something similar. "He loves to express his anger, too, and he uses it very effectively. But he's not an angry guy. If you spend any time with him, he's a lot of fun. But he uses [anger] very effectively." Rebecca Traister writes that releasing anger has personal benefits such as better sleep, appetite, sex, and interpersonal communication. The women say expressing anger is important to their wellness. They can release anger well, which actually seems to decrease how often and intensely they become angry and how long they stay angry.

Sue reflects, "I'm just one person, but I'm not angrier than I was before. I'm probably just as averse to anger, but because of both my upbringing and the community that I'm a part of, I'm not becoming more angry. I'm becoming more strategic and trying to understand where my anger is appropriate and how it should fuel my actions. There's an idea that people become more corrupt when they get power, but I think it's actually that corrupt people are more likely to want power. So, I think that angry people are going to become angrier. I don't think that anger creates angrier people." Sue enacts anger by making herself more strategic, more discerning about where that anger is appropriately directed, and more attentive to right ways for anger to energize her. She does this in the context of other supportive and wise women.

THE ROLE OF COMMUNITY

It takes a community to experience and express anger well. Agapic anger seems to require a set of peers who draw out the best in each other—who cultivate good character through conversations and reflection. People who, along with friends who are mutually focused on the good, work on anger can shape it to become increasingly agapic. Conversely, if one's influencers encourage types or uses of anger that foment hatred, impulsiveness, or violence, then that person's anger can degenerate away from being an agapic, love-filled, or generative force.

Sue reflects, "What is your community? How are your peers helping you keep it in check—use it strategically? One of the things I appreciate about the cultivation around anger I'm getting in the community organizing I'm involved with is that the communities I'm a part of are helping hold me in check, so that the anger I'm using as fuel is not turning to violence; it's not turning to irrationality; it's not turning to rage." Sue's community of other organizers informally helps her form a right relationship with anger, use it well, and remain accountable for the forms of anger to which she assents.

In order to actualize their potential for love, hope, virtuous anger, and courage, people need others to both challenge and affirm their thoughts and actions.[10] Writing about character-forming friends, religious virtue ethicist Cates says,

> Confronting a situation of moral import together, friends communicate to each other initial impressions of value. They encourage each other to reflect upon the moral significance of these impressions. They challenge each other to examine the way in which these impressions have or have not been shaped by more considered moral judgments. They press each other to examine their considered judgments for reasonableness, consistency, and coherence. As they press each other in this fashion, the friends educate each other morally. They also persuade each other mutually toward the shared adoption of a well-deliberated and carefully formulated vision of the good.[11]

The organizers form networks in which they can do the work of co-constructing an ethical vision toward which they work. "Sharing a vision of the good, then, is partly a matter of jointly constructing, by means of continuing reflection and argumentation, an extended network of vision with which to view the world of value."[12] Drea, Sue, Kelly, and Mary, along with other organizers with whom they train and network in addition to the leaders they cultivate in their local settings, share responsibility for the way they envision the good and move toward it. Their vision of the good coming about in this world includes the cultivation of agapic anger and the ongoing reflection on how to use that anger. The women do not surrender to anger in general; they deliberately and rationally are moved with an anger that is rooted in love for a specific reason. They aim at hope for dismantling a specific injustice and/or building toward specific increases in communal justice.

The transformation of angers and the uses of that anger for motivating action for the good of greater justice can occur well only in and through valued relationships. It is only in community, often between an organizer and a leader, but also among organizers themselves, that anger can be identified, critiqued, and properly cultivated. Part of the reason organizers form relationships is indeed because of a shared goal of social transformation. The organizers would not balk at what Aristotle called utility-based friendships that help actualize that goal.

However, their relationships with each other and with the leaders they train move beyond utility. Rather, these relationships often become character friendships of which Aristotle writes that "perfect friendship is the friendship of [women] who are good, and alike in virtue; for these [women] wish well alike to each other qua good, and they are good themselves."[13] Philosophy professor Patrick Lee Miller describes these relationships as ones "between two people who share a feeling of goodwill that is reciprocal, mutually acknowledged, and for the other's sake."[14]

Character friendship depends on the good character of each friend and is important because through engaging in shared deliberation and other activities, they challenge and inspire one another to repeatedly attain to greater good. As Aristotle puts it, character-friends "are thought to become better too by their activities and by improving each other; for from each other they take the mold of the characteristics they approve."[15] Sue recalls an instance when she was angry about something else entirely, but she was able to channel that energy into such incisive clarity that a co-trainer sought her out, "Whatever you were angry about, keep that close when you're training. That was the best I've seen you!" This was not the only time Sue's colleagues have affirmed the clarity that comes out of her anger and, therefore, have invited her to trust and build on this clarity. Whether her friends and colleagues are praising what worked or calling her to a better path next time, they are contributing to her capacity to work with anger and lead well.

A COUNTERPOINT TO THE MOVEMENTS
OF AGAPIC ANGER

Not all anger is agapic. Some harmful tagalongs that are vicious and not known to contribute predictably to communal well-being have been known to hang around anger. Sue is the first, among a small group of women organizers talking together after a day of training, to point out some of the seriously detrimental forms of anger. "I'm thinking about the difference between the kind of anger we're talking about and the kind of anger I see being fueled in our culture now—that is coopting, or taking advantage of, or actually fomenting anger." Pulitzer Prize–winning *New York Times* reporter Charles Duhigg notices something similar. "America has always been an angry nation. We are a country born of revolution. . . . Recently, however, the tenor of our anger has shifted. It has become less episodic and more persistent, a constant drumbeat in our lives. It is directed less often at people we know and more often at distant groups that are easy to demonize."[16]

Sue digs deeper, "I do wonder about anger—that it really is being used *against* the people who are alone, and some of the people who are alone are using their anger in ways that are just making them more isolated. I am not in any way saying we shouldn't tap into anger. It's definitely a tool. But, right now, I also think there's a danger in our culture about how it's being used and exploited by people for their own needs—people who aren't necessarily angry; they're just [greedy]."

Nods of agreement encircle the table, other women recognizing the concern that anger can be misused and harmful. Drea gives an example. "I was thinking about youth—thinking about Chicago and our violence—and I think that a lot of our youth are angry, and they will automatically go from one to ten in a heartbeat and not use the tools of negotiation, or listening, or even like your fists. They're picking up weapons, and it's like their anger shouts: 'Well, I'm angry at you, so I'm gonna *show you* I'm angry at you. I'm gonna get revenge!'"

Hearing Drea's story, Mary expresses compassion for young people and accuses national figures of being poor role models. "[Anger is] being used [by a certain politician] in the country to promote outrage. So many people say, 'What's happening to young people?'" She delivers the next line with an edge of sarcasm: "Well, they've got great models at the national level. Right? How do we dare ask what's happened to our young people when we permit our leaders, our judges, and our Congress, and our president to use the most vile language about other people? So, I think that's a level at which anger is being promoted, and it's violent anger being promoted. It's not rooted in anything other than, 'Be careful because *they're* going to take yours. You know, they're going to take your share of the pie and you've got to stop 'em.' And who are the 'they'? They are young people. They're Black people. They're brown people. They're immigrants. They're the poor. They're the seniors. They're the children. Those are the 'they.'" Breeding discontent, attacking vulnerable people, turning to violence, and promoting incivility constitute offensive uses of anger in the eyes of the women.

Reflecting at a later time, Sue adds, "Although I value anger, I am also aware that it is addictive; certain types of anger are addictive. And I think that one of the problems we're having in our country is that people are angry, and they're addicted to that feeling. And they're taking it out in all kinds of inappropriate ways—where people are being reinforced and rewarded and encouraged to use their anger to be violent, to be exclusivists, to be racist. Some of these communities are white supremacist communities that are coming out being violent against other people, or individuals who are shooting other people. I think people are trying to get another hit of that—the addictive part is the spark—without learning to wait for the cooldown—for the strategic, 'How could this be better for my community, and my country?'" Sue adds that organizers oppose anger that culminates in aggression, violence, lack of control, or other nonstrategic behaviors.

The women only act upon anger that has a prosocial solution in sight. Therefore, Drea cautions against "the anger where people can't see past red, where they go break windows and tear up things to make other people angry. It's problematic when there's no solution to their anger, there's no hope, there's no answer, there's no one to be there for them. I think youth being alone and angry is dangerous. They need mentorship. They need guidance. They need somebody to show them there's hope. And that goes for adults, too. If there's no solution, or there's no eyes on the prize, they're going to stay in their anger." For the most part, Drea identifies here the need for anger to be oriented toward a good solution, which is a cooled-off kind of anger, before acting on it. However, she also seems to note what a mature and difficult skill this is and how hard it is to accomplish it alone. Isolation and anger tend to be a toxic combination.

There are four problems the remainder of this chapter will expose; surely the reader will add more. First, there are things that are not anger but feed on anger or get mislabeled as anger in our culture. Second, people's capacity to delude themselves as to their true motivations complicates working effectively with anger. Third, there is an enormous difference between various species of anger—agapic anger, to which the women assent, and other vicious forms of anger they exclude. Fourth, anger's transmutability makes it susceptible to going awry.

The first of these problems is that things get labeled as anger that are not themselves anger. First and foremost, think of violence. Violence differs greatly from anger, but in our culture it can be treated as synonymous with anger. Violence is an action intended to hurt, whereas anger is an emotion. Agapic anger doesn't just reject violence; it refuses even to edge down the pathway toward violence. Even fomenting people's anger to a fever-pitch is excluded. Consider *Beauty and the Beast*'s Gaston stirring up the mob—or other people whipping up mob-mentality even when only a fraction of the mob have physical harm in mind. Gaston feeds the townspeople lies about the Beast that incite both fear and anger in them. He foments people's anger, exploits it for the leader's goal, and decreases people's agency by inciting the mob to stay in the *furor* (explosive) or *fel* (manufactured) anger while withholding the conditions under which people deliberate well. Even if violence is not anger, violence does seem to feed on blameworthy forms of anger. Leaders who choreograph good anger do not assent to pathways that consider violence.

Second, there's a lot of pressure to be seen as a good person—a pressure religious contexts can exacerbate. Most people want to interpret their own motivations as ethically superlative. Researchers call it the "overconfidence bias," which applies not only to intellect and how fast you get things done, but also to matters of character. People "assume that they have good character and will therefore do the right thing when they encounter ethical challenges."[17] How does this apply to doing anger well? Agapic anger requires making accurate assessments about causes, motives, and goals surrounding a hurtful occurrence. Yet people tend to think they are better at recalling and assessing the event than statistics bear out. Therefore, when people recall the cause of their anger, they are cognitively likely to underestimate the negative contribution they may have made and overestimate fault that lies with others. When assessing their own motivations for being angry, people are likely to describe the most flattering version, which is often less accurate than a more fulsome, complicated version. Or people can deceive themselves that their anger benefits the widest swath of humanity, when really it is just what they want. Finally, when naming the goal of anger, people can trick themselves into thinking it virtuous, even when it is actually payback in sheep's clothing. "Excessive faith in ourselves and our abilities makes it harder for us to see how prone we are to errors and biases."[18] Overconfidence bias makes it easy to be misguided about our own degree of honesty and blamelessness. Even if anger is, by definition, a response to a perceived injustice and aims at its correction, people can be (and often are) mistaken in their ideas about what is just. When they are mistaken, their anger will likely fall short of virtue.

Third, agapic anger differs greatly from other angers. The women pass over forms of anger that can foment public disdain, become a means of controlling others, focus on the wrong cause, get expressed more intensely than is warranted, be harbored for an unfitting duration of time, and so on. As Schnell and Cates note, forms of anger are fluid, and "although we have specified some different forms of anger, experiences of them should be viewed as porous. Each of them can easily overlap or flow into and out of another as the details of situations change."[19]

Fourth, angers morph from one form to another or even into adjacent emotions as my brilliant (really) colleague Diana Fritz Cates and I explored in our article, "Rethinking Anger as a Desire for Payback."[20] The experiential and biochemical proximity of various forms of anger makes assenting to any anger a process requiring caution due to the very real possibilities of starting out employing anger well only to find oneself sliding into a neighboring form of anger that one does not rationally accept as appropriate. Although the capacity of emotions to morph is a wonder of the adaptive potential of humans, the fluidity of anger is a reason for caution. Anger to which a person initially may do well to assent can shift into an anger, camouflaged and hard to detect, that one does well to refuse.

CHAPTER SIX

Social Transformation

Shaping Anger to Benefit Communities

Working with anger is a sort of dance—a set of movements—that helps people shape anger toward the good. Shaping anger matters on at least three levels. On the structural and institutional level, anger can increase the potency of social justice movements. On the interpersonal plane, anger can help form resilient leaders. On the personal level, it helps people know themselves better, which enables them to form better habits with their anger.

A theory of choreography can help show how such transformations of anger work. Choreographers direct the movements of other people. They compose with specific dancers and actors in mind, make mutually informed adjustments along the way, and then expect people to adhere to the choreography they designed. In addition, choreographers equip people to have precise and prearranged movements down by a certain performance date. Yet, for social choreography the iterative process of practicing movements is the point, with transformation of a life a primary goal and transformation of some unjust systems an adjacent goal.

MOVEMENTS OF PROSOCIAL TRANSFORMATION

Emotions are movements—internal changes that are evoked by mostly sensory impressions—and the transformation of anger entails certain interior changes. Transformation of anger includes some self-directed internal realignment through the formation of habits and dispositions. Finally, transforming systems, partially through a cultivation around anger, requires concrete change—movement wrought in some social structure or system so there is prosocial change in people's circumstances. Choreography helps envision how movements—internal and external—build, convey, and transform the emotions and actions of participants. Choreographing anger can bring about transformation in at least at three places in a person's life: one's own anger, relationships with ideas, struggles, or other people, and harmful institutional and social structures that limit one's flourishing.

Susan Leigh Foster, who defines choreography as "ways of structuring movement . . . both the kinds of actions performed and their sequence or progression,"[1] argues that choreographies shape the people who move through their steps, saying choreographic form leaves its "trace in the bodies that had performed it."[2] She is highlighting the impression of choreography on the bodies of those who enact it. Foster makes clear that choreography leaves traces on audiences as well as those who perform it.

Choreography has a history of leaving traces on populations by enacting prosocial transformation. Foster argues that the body is "a vast reservoir of signs and symbols" capable of persuasion and resistance.[3] Bodies' fluid participation in social choreographies of protest can make public claims that converse with, defy, or reorient cultural norms and practices. Foster develops "a new perspective on individual agency and collective action, one that casts the body in a central role as enabling human beings to work together to create social betterment."[4] Looking at three grassroots protests— 1960s lunch counter sit-ins, 1980s ACT-UP die-ins, and the 1999 protests of the World Trade Organization in Seattle—she argues that individual and social agency is not simply expressed in bodily movement, it is partly constituted in and through bodily movement. Choreography gets people's bodies in positions of rebuttals to injustice and a brighter imagined future is enacted.[5]

Professor of dance history and theory Rebekah Kowal's work shows "correlations between the gradual redefinition among choreographers of dance as a form of ordinary movement, and the growing sense among members of the general public (including dancers) of the power of movement to conduct progressive social change."[6] Kowal finds that dance and social choreographies alike catalyze social and cultural transformation.[7] The power of bodies in motion to constitute needed social change was enacted, argues Kowal, in many and various ways by both dancers and civil rights activists in the 1960s. In social choreographies, such as the Greensboro sit-ins at the F. W. Woolworth's five-and-dime store, activists let action critique daily life, demanding liberative movement in policies and practices.[8] Kowal also challenges conventional notions that choreography has to be prescribed. For example, she says that improvisational forms build given and unexpected circumstances into choreography in real time with litheness and ingenuity.[9]

The improvisational choreography described by Kowal pertains to the shaping of anger. There is no predetermined script. When one, in the context of mentoring or spiritual care, notices the presence (or unprincipled absence[10]) of anger, organizers extemporize and may take up the opportunity for transformation. When inviting people to transform their anger, the process is nonlinear; it is improvisational. It is less about scripting precise movements in advance than it is reconceiving the order of movements anew in real time with each person, depending on their needs. In many cases, it may not feel like facilitating a process intentionally at all. Rather, in phronesis—practical wisdom—as deacons, pastors, or organizers build relationships aimed at cultivating transformed and transformative leaders in relation to social change, they recognize that certain leaders are ready to transform their anger into good, so they help leaders take steps in that direction. Thus, a choreography of anger fits the improvisational form to which Kowal refers.

Choreographed by religious leaders and performed by congregational and community participants, good anger both makes an impression on the systems at which it is aimed *and* makes an indelible, embodied impression on the people who participate in transforming their anger. By making an impression on systems, it thereby makes impressions on additional people, even if they do not witness the process personally.

PULLED IN TWO DIRECTIONS

A complicated aspect of any anger and, therefore, also of agapic anger is that it simultaneously moves in two directions. With anger, a person simultaneously tends away from the cause of anger—some harm perceived as contrary to her goodness (e.g., the person who caused injury), and she also tends toward the goal of anger—a perceived good (e.g., right resolution).[11] Angered people focus part of their attention on a perceived slight and part on a good that can be achieved by confronting and challenging the slight.

Note that the "harm" and the "good" aspects are interrelated; people's anger moves in two directions at once. In general, anger recoils from specific violations of justice and moves toward some specific change that would bring about increased communal good. Aquinas's moral philosophy of the twofold pull of anger, namely that people experiencing anger tend away from a cause viewed "under the aspect of evil" and toward a goal viewed "under the aspect of good" maps onto an organizing training segment: "World as it is; world as it could be." "The world as it is" helps groups unearth what they see as wrong in the world—what repulses them "under the aspect of evil." It identifies things that keep people from shared flourishing, living their full humanity, or developing their capacities. People can decide to work *against* such perceived evils.

Organizers help people think about the "world as it could be" so people can name a hoped-for reality they deem possible—what they are drawn toward "under the aspect of good." This is the good and eschatological world God continues creating. Naming prosocial realities people envision for their communities clarifies what they love and therefore pinpoints what their anger might tend toward. This process of discernment illumines the sort of social transformation that would be consistent with the group's values—what they love. Sue offers an example of a car speeding through the neighborhood that put one's grandkids at risk. This might look like getting clear that one's love is for the child, which makes one repelled by a speeding car that puts the child at risk and makes working toward speed bumps that protect children's safety a goal.

Kelly says the "world as it is" helps people identify "the things wrong with the world. . . . [The people being trained] name what they see wrong in the world." It will differ group to group since local burdens, pressures, and issues vary. Kelly, who developed leaders among multiple congregations, explains, "One congregation might articulate that they are seeing a lot of broken families and elders being isolated, and they name the systemic sin like that. If I went to [another] congregation, they might say climate change and injustice against LGBT people, and that's how they see brokenness in the world. So, regardless of what the faith tradition is, they name how they see it." This helps groups identify the system against which they work—the harm their anger moves away from.

Having named what is wrong with the world as it is, the training turns to the "world as it should be." "This is what our faith values tell us it should be." This is the world with the goodness God created it to have. Kelly says it is foundational to be able to "imagine the world differently than it is today [because then] you can operate from a place of hope. You can't have the hope unless at the core you know that there is a behavior that is happening, and it can be changed." Thus, the women help people to articulate the sort of transformation they seek. Kelly says, "I just orient them: 'So if you believe it *can* be different, then what do we do about it?' Anyone who's in an organizing role will orient them toward moving because we can see the world differently. And we know that in order for that difference to occur, we have to do something." They may decide to organize *toward* what they deem necessary for communal human flourishing.

The "world as it is, world as it should be" training uncovers the double movements of anger so that groups harness what is needed for action. Kelly summarizes: "If you can't mobilize around that anger—the thing that says that this is not right [world as it is] and knowing that it could be different [world as it should be]—then you can't have hope."

Organizers invite reflection on the gap between current practices and a more just society that they can envision. They ask, "What could right a wrong in this case? What could restore the world toward right?" The women help people to appreciate both their aversion to some abusive system operative in the "world as it is" and their desire for some particular social transformation congruent with the "world as it could be." These are, in fact, the two directions of anger's movement.

RECOILING FROM ABUSIVE SYSTEMS

Mary notes that people need to be allowed to have anger about a violation of something they care about, and she gives a particular example. "I talk about my own anger and why I'm so angry. I say, 'It's directly related to a violation. . . . How do you think Jesus felt when he threw the money changers out of the temple? What was his emotion? Did he say, "Would you please . . .; If you don't mind . . .; Would you please leave because I feel a little bit offended"? What do you think?' [*pause . . .*] He screamed and yelled at them and maybe even kicked them in the ass! I mean I don't know, but what do you think his emotion was like? What was he feeling when he demanded that they leave the temple? And why? What was the violation? People [need to] begin to connect and say, 'Well, Jesus could get angry. Right? I guess I can get angry.' And part of the problem is that we're trained, especially women, to eat our anger—to just live with it. Right?

"We don't want people punching people, but we want people to feel justified anger when something they care about gets violated. You have an absolute right to be angry about that. Absolute right!" Mary points to a specific violation that angered Jesus: the temple's corrupt economic system harming many people. His anger at that violation impels him to drive out money changers. More than this, it drives him to make a statement about all forms of economic corruption that benefit a few at the expense of many, forms that purport to benefit all but do not. Mary wants people to know that they, like Jesus, can feel indignant about particular abuse and call out the related abusive system.

Regarding what Kelly's anger is about, she replies, "I only think about it in specifics." Asked what those specifics include, Kelly answers without missing a beat: "Gross misuse of power. Gross negligence—like willful ignorance. Sexism. Systemic injustice." What Kelly reels off as "specifics" are each massive overarching issues of violation; yet, each has very particular instantiations in her experience.

For example, after naming systemic injustice, Kelly refers to a story in which their church voted to continue discriminating against people who identify as LGBTQIA+. "I didn't know anything of polity then. I was young; I was in my twenties, and I was new to the Methodist Church, so I didn't know much about how it all worked. But what I learned was that there was a small group of people who had set up the rules, and not everyone had a voice in that. And if I were around during the time that it was set up, I wouldn't have had a voice in it, even if I really wanted to. And my husband probably would not have had a voice in it either. And so, we realized that the people who ought to be heard and be able to share their experience were not allowed at the table. And that was inherently wrong."

Even within this story, Kelly is repulsed by three enormous, abusive systems: sexism, racism, and discrimination based on sexual orientation. It is not that she is repelled by faceless, intractable issues; she is repelled by particular situations that she relates to larger systems (in this case of discrimination). The harm away from which anger moves is specific for each of us, and at the same time it is tied to systemic issues.

Moving toward Social Transformation

Recoiling from abusive systems is only part of anger's movement; crucially, anger also moves toward social transformation. With anger, one does not settle for feeling disturbed by what is contrary to human well-being. Rather, importantly, anger gets to simultaneously progress toward some transformation in order to build toward the just world that people want to live in. Social transformation means an ongoing change that operates on the communal level, aiming at shared human flourishing, which seeks the active enjoyment of the most good possible by the largest number of people possible, preferentially attending to the voices and the needs of people who are poor and oppressed. This definition of social transformation is quite similar to what Paul Woodruff identifies as the goal of justice: "the flourishing of the community through the flourishing of each of its members."[12]

Sue, Kelly, Mary, and Drea have worked toward specific social transformations such as racial diversity on institutional boards, the well-being of children relative to housing security, racial equity in the structure of congregations, increased access to safe methods for opioid disposal, and for more general social transformation toward reducing suffering, restoring justice, and maintaining justice. The social transformation they seek aims at the world as it could be were things set right. Anger tends toward this hoped-for reality they view as good, and they organize toward this "good" they love.

The women do not aim to reach an ideal society so much as they aim to lead communities in the participatory activity of continual transformation in the direction of greater justice and happiness, especially for people who have long been oppressed and have suffered unspeakable pain. The transformation the women seek occurs partly in and through working with others in their communities to get clear about what they love and to habituate their anger itself to be loving, hopeful, and cool so that it can consistently help to motivate wise and effective action. The cooperative transformation of anger has value in itself and is not only tied to an end goal.

Transformation focuses on *building* better systems, which is an incremental and iterative process that is realized across spans of time. However, building often necessarily involves *dismantling* unjust systems because part of restoring right is changing what is wrong. The discussion of dismantling systems is included here, as a portion of "moving toward social transformation" rather than earlier on the topic of "recoiling from abusive systems" because dismantling is regarded by the women as a positive step in bringing about the world as it could be.

In reality the movements of aversion to abusive systems and the desire for change are intertwined and not tidily separated. Building and dismantling simply are interwoven. Let's say the justice one seeks is affordable housing in Chicago. Building toward justice might entail fighting to keep one development in one neighborhood zoned for a certain percentage of affordable housing. If developers want it rezoned for more affluent housing and hold undue sway over the city council, then the pursuit of justice may require dismantling the council and helping to elect leaders who are motivated to preserve affordable housing.

Moving toward social transformation, although right and good, can involve high tension because it often requires dismantling unjust systems that benefit a relatively few privileged people at the expense of many vulnerable people. Dismantling injustice, even if the disassembling is partial, is usually painful for those who are benefiting from the unjust arrangement of power and goods because it involves the loss of inequitable personal and social power. The organizers, therefore, have to accept that people who benefit from abusive systems may encounter pain as a byproduct of increased justice. Some reflective people will notice not only did they lose something they valued highly, such as privilege or a higher payout, but they also participated in wrongdoing by supporting a harmful system.

People who lose power as a result of the dismantling of unjust social structures could feel that they are suffering payback—even unjust payback. On the contrary, deconstruction would amount to payback only if the goal of anger were the suffering of the abuser or of those maintaining abusive systems. If, however, the goal of anger unwaveringly remains dismantling for the sake of a greater good, then dismantling does not constitute payback. When the women use anger in their work, they do not focus on causing the abusers to suffer; rather, they focus on removing unjust causes of suffering for the many, the vulnerable. Here again caution is necessary, however, for even if a person begins dismantling for the sake of justice, the process of dismantling could morph into less praiseworthy goals associated with more problematic forms of anger.

From the women's perspectives, they want in their anger to constrain the freedom of abusers for the purpose of liberating the oppressed. Often, they desire redress as well. Ideally a person who had limited others' flourishing could learn empathy and come to promote the common good, which would move beyond redress and toward restoration. For example, a politician who has been blocking affordable housing legislation could learn empathy through the process of redress and come to promote the well-being of people dealing with housing insecurity. For an organizer, such reform-oriented goals are rational if there is cause to think the goals can be achieved. The women rarely deem idyllic goals likely to be achieved. Therefore, they rarely select one person's change as their aim because changing that one person who inhabits a privileged position is less important to them than is changing the circumstances for masses of people who inhabit less privileged positions. Also, the organizers do not need that one individual to change personally so much as they need the system or legislation to change. For example, they need the politician's vote, not that politician's internal awakening to empathy, although the latter would be welcome.

PART III

Virtue Ethics of Agapic Anger

Practicing beneficial dispositions in relation to anger generates good and powerful formation regarding how to perceive reality, draw conclusions about people and situations, determine a desirable pace of responsiveness, select desired outcomes, and respond, and so on. Such practices condition and modify anger.

The basics of virtue ethics are laid out in chapter 8. The chapter discusses how the formative power of habits can dispose people "to do justice and to love kindness and to walk humbly with your God" (Micah 6:8). Then the chapter turns toward showing how, from a virtue ethics perspective, anger could be a good habit for faith-filled people. Here the chapter takes a theoretical turn—describing a virtue ethics of anger through which people can be moved by anger to feel well, deliberate well, and do well. This chapter delivers the mechanics of how to sense and feel things aptly, and how to cultivate emotions that tell the truth about reality. While the chapter teaches how to consistently reason well about issues of ethical import and to increase agency through thoughtfulness, it also describes how to reliably come through with value-aligned actions. Finally, from the perspective of virtue ethics, agapic anger is assessed as good.

Chapter 9 discusses several ways that anger can be vicious. The women's stories show a type of truth-telling that yielded four specific cautions. Their stories show ways to enact philosophies and thoughtful practices that address limitations in Aristotle and Aquinas's writings on anger. These women have practiced living with decolonial, antiracist, and feminist values, which means they know some things that Aristotle and Aquinas did not.

Sue's narrative in chapter 7 shows ways that she asks questions about nuancing the use of anger and considers anger's problems. Her story explores questions about the limitations of anger's helpfulness and its potential allegiance to harmful behaviors. Some people get to express anger while it is not permitted for others. Power analyses help reveal who gets to be angry, as well as when and how anger is deemed acceptable.

CHAPTER SEVEN

Becoming the Leaders God Intends

Meet Sue Engh

Bicycle helmet tucked under her arm, sweat decorating her brow, Sue Engh steps into Maeve's Café and in easy strides crosses the length of this local, woman-owned coffee house in Northeast Minneapolis—her vigor matched only by the pools of serenity that somehow gather around her. Sue chose this place on recommendation—a spot known for its focus on social justice.

On Higgins Road in the northwest suburbs of Chicago, an expansive brick façade has lifted a tall cross into the sky since 1966, eight years after Prince of Peace Lutheran Church was chartered. Between her childhood home and church lay an oft-crossed, grassy field. "I was close to my pastors growing up. I had really good pastors . . . so I spent time [at church] outside of Sundays." Sue knew her church inside and out; eager and proficient, she jumped in to help when little things came up.

Sue incisively cuts to the narrow demographics of this place where she had grown up. I lived "in a fairly middle-upper class neighborhood—community, family, church. White. Very white." Prince of Peace and Hoffman Estates largely were populated with people of various European descents. Of her family of origin, Sue acknowledges, "We're Scandinavian; entirely. White food. White people. Very even keel emotions—at least from what I saw. Tension was not something you cultivated. Anger was not something you cultivated." Sue was rewarded in certain ways for being a peacemaker in the family. Such a reward structure "keeps anger really at bay. Not only are you supposed to not get angry, but you have to make sure that everybody else is getting along—not getting angry at each other." Partially handed this role, partially taking it upon herself, Sue is sure that she got angry at times but recalls expressing it in tears, which made for some confusion. "If I would cry, I usually thought I must be sad, but I might actually have been angry—didn't know how to express it other than tears." When she cried, someone would be there for her, so there was a way in which tears as an expression of anger got reinforced. As she looks back on it, she finds "I'm becoming clearer that part of white culture is anger avoidance—or at least for women. I think that was something I wasn't aware of at the time."

As a kid, she did pick up on displays of anger being more acceptable for some people than for others. Specifically, her dad, who she loves and affirms and whose affirmation she coveted growing up, was permitted anger. Although she knew he was a safe person, he was also "a big guy, and loud. So, when [my dad] got mad at me or anything, it was scary. Not only that there was this big person who was shouting, but what does that mean for our relationship? . . . My dad would recognize [the volume and magnitude of his anger] a little way into the tantrum he was having, and then he would—he never left us—but he would disappear, like emotionally, or sometimes he would walk out of the house, which I think was probably wise on his part, but for me it was like, 'Now he's gone! He's withdrawn from us.' It was clear that his anger was permissible, but hard for us all to take. And my mom was very submissive, so I would also watch that aspect of things. But [she was] deeply committed to my dad, so she would never talk negatively about it—never challenged him on his reactions to things." Sue's dad's rare bursts of verbalized anger taught her, below the level of conscious processing, that there were dangers associated with expressing anger. Even though her dad was occasionally angry, anger was not a predominant emotion. "Rather, kindness and generosity were [my parents'] strong suits. Even [Dad] discouraged the rest of us from feeling or expressing anger. I always felt that part of that had to do with their faith and what they believed God was like and what God expected of God's people."

Part-way through her work in organizing, Sue came to develop a complex understanding of anger, so that her early awareness of its danger was augmented by experiences of the necessity and benefit of certain, specific enactments of anger. After years of conversation, action, and reflection, Sue now recognizes the basis of her own anger, into which she at times needs to tap. "The source of my anger has to do with being denied—systematically denied—by patriarchy, but specifically, [by] my own father or colleagues in my life who have been in charge of something that I want access to: a role in the church or authority in my preaching or something like that. . . . It mostly has to do with male privilege and males in my life who have made me believe that I am less than." Without actually believing she was less, Sue can see that there were times she accepted the role of the lesser and cooperated in her oppression.

THIS BEAUTIFUL, BROKEN, BELOVED CHURCH

Looking back, a clear trajectory forms—from elementary and teenage years spending free time at Prince of Peace, to summer camp counselor jobs, to youth director positions, to the pastorate, to faith-based community organizing. "I'm a deeply ecclesial and theological person. My framework is ecclesial. I mean I'm a church geek. I tell my kids I have confirmation with now—I tell them, 'I loved confirmation!' They just roll their eyes. From a very early age I was really drawn to a theological perspective on things and a deep love for the church."

Steadfast love for the church and a penchant for theological thinking led Sue, after seminary, to serve a small inner-city church in Minneapolis. One of her roles was outreach, but how she (and the congregation) thought about outreach changed over time. At first "most of us would be like, 'We need more members in our congregation,' and, 'We want to get to know our neighbors.'" Despite neighborhood door knocking, inviting people to church, and welcoming neighbors to church events, the congregation was shrinking. At the same time, "we were also becoming aware of more partners in the neighborhood. In the later—second half—of my tenure there, we began to get to know a neighborhood group that was looking for space and we were looking for renters. So, we opened up part of our space and began to get to know this neighborhood organization and started to understand a little more what neighborhood organizing is. That began to open my eyes to being participants or players in the life of our community—not just, 'Who wants to be a part of our church?'"

Next Sue took a call to an affluent, suburban congregation with a big staff. "Part of my new call was to help this new congregation discover something other than charity." The congregation leaders recognized that their church "had been a very generous congregation in terms of charity. But there were some there who believed there must be more than charity. And it was very coincidental or a God thing—that was really where I was at in my journey, too."

Sue already had two pastoral mentors who had been involved in community organizing. She sat down with them, excitedly detailing her call to move beyond a charity model and acknowledging, "I don't know how to do it." These mentors had cofounded a neighborhood organization that would eventually merge with a St. Paul and a St. Cloud organization, becoming "ISAIAH"—a Gamaliel (recall the organization Mary and Greg started) affiliate. "Right away they said, 'Oh, you need to meet this organizer. . . . You need to go to training.'" So early in Sue's tenure at this suburban church, she attended a Gamaliel training, where Mary Gonzales was one of the first trainers to agitate her around who she really wanted to be. "Also, serendipitously [ISAIAH] was just trying to move out of being an urban organization solely and thinking about a metropolitan approach to the issues they were working on. So, they were looking for suburban congregations. And they were looking for big ones in part because they needed the funding." The local ISAIAH organizer "saw a congregation he wanted in and a leader who could do that." He mentored Sue as she developed an organizing orientation in a congregation that had focused on charity. "Over that seven and a half years that I was there, I got my congregation involved in what was becoming ISAIAH, sent a number of leaders to training, got involved in the clergy caucus of ISAIAH, got *very active* in the clergy caucus and went to a lot of different trainings myself—first a seven-day training, and then went to an advanced clergy training, several over those seven years. I did a lot of *being* trained."

Then Sue was called into fulltime faith-based community organizing positions. After about seven years of including organizing practices in congregational ministry, she applied for the ISAIAH organizer position and, amid competition, got it. Years later, as one of the few Lutheran community organizers in the United States, Sue knew about the open director of community organizing position at the Evangelical Lutheran Church in America (ELCA). Created just six years before, that position was now vacant. She applied and got it.

This job moved her work back to Chicago—a place where she already had friends, family, and a sense of the area. She developed relationships with leaders across the nation and focused on the program *Vital Congregations, Just Communities*. She recruited eighteen synods (regional bodies in the ELCA) into this program to revitalize through three-day community organizing trainings. In order to facilitate these trainings across the country, she created a network of organizers local to each synod. "The idea was to expose people to this idea. If they wanted to do more, they could go to a seven-day training. We covered some of the basic, entry-level ideas. That was the bulk of my first two years." In the next years, she promoted awareness of community organizing in the ELCA by being out in congregations and synods inspiring and educating people to get involved in faith-based initiatives for sustained social change.

During her eleven years as director for community organizing, she also developed a cohort of faith leaders interested in extending organizing trainings and networking for transformation. "I was meeting people at ELCA 'developer trainings'—missional training events" and teaching leaders how to do one-to-ones. "Some of them would come up to me and say, 'We need to just be doing a lot more of these kinds of trainings at these events.'" While she was not in the position to change the developer trainings, she did notice and respond to a pattern. "When we were having one of these events, three other people came up to me and said the same thing." She responded, "'I think you need to meet each other. I'm going to create an event and get some of these people from around the country together and see what they want to do with that.' So, in 2010 we had the first one in Minneapolis right after one of those missional leadership trainings; many of them had to come to that anyway." Fifteen people from five ministries came. "I got some local organizers I still knew from ISAIAH to come do the training. I crafted an agenda that would create relationships, talk about best and worst practices, and just ask them, 'What more do you want?' 'Do you want to meet again?' It was overwhelmingly, 'Yes!'" From that point on, Sue secured funding to gather leaders usually two times per year. Funding the bulk of it was important for leaders because there "were a lot of young people with a lot of college debt or congregations that didn't want to send their pastors to yet one more thing that they had to pay for." She told trainees, "This cohort [is] a way for you all to [get] to know each other and start to strategize together around the tools of organizing and contextual ministry." She is adamant that organizing "is not just about tools: it's actually about transformation. It's about transforming people's lives and transforming or forming us into the kinds of disciples, the kinds of leaders that God intends for us to be. So I guess I want to just put that seed in your brain that, yes, these are very practical tools, but think about how much more exciting this work is if it's about transformation—[about] your own and about the people that God puts in front of you and next to you and about your congregation, the ministries in your communities! That just makes it all the more exciting and animating." Organizing calls people into relationships and action around their self-interest. In organizing, self-interest means valuing themselves while caring about others around them. This includes people's "passions, their dreams, their hopes, their struggles—something that you have heard them talk about or know about them because of your relationship with them, something that will meet them where they are and bring them some satisfaction."

Across her years in organizing, Sue's understanding of anger has expanded; yet she retains a warranted wariness toward anger, recognizing that, while anger can function for good, it undeniably also can malfunction. "I have intellectually shifted how I perceive anger, but it has been almost impossible for me to shift to actually *embrace* it. I've usually had people point out to me when they see my anger coming forward in a way that's helpful. Like my first [ISAIAH] organizer—and still a good colleague—has more than once said to me, 'When you're angry, you're a good trainer.' Or he'll just say, 'Get in touch with your anger about such and such because I think that will help you get clear.' I remember when I visited [my daughter] when she was doing her semester in South America. I came back after visiting her, having seen the poverty, and having seen the governmental oppression and corruption, and [having] some sense of how the US has contributed to that, and just feeling really angry about the results. When I came back and was telling my staff about it—that's when I was working at ISAIAH—and he said, 'Wow! I hope you can tap into that anger when you're training or when you're leading an event. . .' So, it usually has to be pointed out to me: A) that I'm angry, and B) how to channel it in a way that can be helpful. When I'm angry, I can be clearer and more powerful. If I can get in touch with it, I can be more dynamic. [I'm] never totally embracing 'Oh Yeah! I'm gonna build on this!'"

"I'm pretty clear now that I'm really angry about what we're doing to immigrants and families and children—partly because there's nothing clearer to me in the Bible that we are called to be outraged about—how the stranger is treated because all people are God's people. I'm actually so angry about it that I'm motivated to find an immigration lawyer and say, 'Okay, is there some way that my skill set can be a part of this mission?'"

"I'm [also] really angry about race relations and racism and white privilege. And right now, one of the ways I'm most angry about it is our criminal justice system. And again, just trying to figure out, how do you wedge yourself in there and be some part of changing a narrative or changing a reality? Most people don't believe they're racists. And I don't want to believe I'm racist, but we're behaving in racist ways by not *seeing* what it is we do that's contributing. We could help people see the injustices and get angry about them—even angry that they're participating."

Ever processing at multiple levels, Sue adds, "I don't want to turn a bunch of people on themselves—'Oh, I'm such a bad person; I'm contributing to that!' Sometimes we have to go through that. Unfortunately, sometimes we then turn our anger back on ourselves. For a while that's okay: 'Yeah, I'm a sinner too.' 'Boy, I didn't . . .' But then [we need] to do something with it that changes both me—the way I behave—and perhaps how things play out in my culture. So, I think anger can have a role in moving someone to a different behavior so that a different map of reality is created."

NOTICING JESUS'S ANGER

Biblical texts contributed to Sue's early formation to avoid anger; at the same time the Bible has had a primary role in her reevaluation of anger and openness toward specific sorts of anger. In her youth, Sue memorized two biblical passages that contributed to her suspicion of anger and that still come easily to mind. James 1:19–20 "came into my memory bank at an impressionable time. It was probably my sophomore or junior year in high school, and we were at Bible camp and our counselor was someone who I especially adored. She taught us this passage early that week and had us memorize it: 'You must understand this, my beloved: let everyone be quick to listen, slow to speak, slow to anger; for your anger does not produce God's righteousness.' Each day we would take time during Bible study to examine different parts of the passage and be challenged to live it during our time at camp." That passage "does, in fact, tell us not to become angry at all if we want to stay within God's righteousness. Well, I loved my counsellor; I loved camp. So, part of it was, 'I'm going to be a dutiful Christian; I'm going to please my counsellor. This is really wise stuff for a Christian to know.'" The other example that came to mind was from Ephesians 4:26: "'Don't let the sun go down on your anger.'"

The idea that you shouldn't let anger fester beyond the setting of the sun, that always has stuck with me." Ever curious and thoughtful, Sue pondered in real time: "What I just now realized is that I have never thought about the line that precedes the Ephesians quote above, which is 'Be angry, but do not sin . . .' Hmmm. Why didn't anyone ever teach me that part? It clearly indicates that 'being angry' is not wrong in and of itself. It's what you do with—or how you express—your anger that could lead you to sin."

Sue's intimate and evolving relationship with biblical texts and interpretation moved the needle over time on her understanding of anger. "Through most of my life, I understood that anger was an *appropriate* response for God to have toward God's human creatures. Especially in the Old Testament, there are many times that God seems to get angry, but maybe I thought, 'God's allowed to do that; and God's not going to lose control.' Although sometimes God does lose control! Or almost does unless someone talks God out of it. . . . And at times I saw the appropriate angry attitude of some of God's chosen agents, such as the prophets."

"For a long time, the only *positive* impression about anger that I got from the gospels had to do with Jesus's cleansing of the temple, when he turned over the tables. In fact, I was under the false assumption that this was the only time when he got really angry. But later in life—and significantly, after I'd entered into the realm of community organizing—an organizer colleague, who is also a pastor [and] an organizer with ISAIAH in South Africa, challenged me on this assumption. He asked me, 'Did Jesus ever get angry?' I said, 'Well yeah, that one time.' And he agitated me. He said, 'You've got to go back and read your Bible.' And that was really hard to take because I pride myself on knowing the Bible. He said, 'Look at how many times you think Jesus was at least kind of simmering. And if not [on the surface] then simmering under the surface.' So, I hardly had to go back and read. I just had to think again because I know the Bible pretty well. I'd been avoiding the idea that anger was something that Jesus could have regularly, or that it could have any useful place. When I started looking at Jesus's anger, my eyes were opened to the reality of his angry reactions to many different people and things he experienced. I realized it was not just strategic—it was heartfelt—but it was right, and it was good, and it had a role and a purpose. This realization helped me to gain a much more helpful attitude about anger, and willingness to acknowledge my own in a more positive light."

When training people, instead of pointing to "places in the Bible where anger is used, I tend to say, 'Doesn't that story make you angry?' Especially around stories about women—abuse and rape and dismemberment—how that's been brushed under the carpet, or rationalized, or symbolized. I'm interested in getting people to be angry about something that's unjust—and [free them to see] 'Here's an example of it in Scripture.' or, 'Elijah or Jesus, or so and so got angry about that, can you understand why?' I look at where Jesus is agitating people. One I like to talk about is the prophet Nathan agitating David—telling him a story and really sucking him in, then landing the punchline: 'You're the man.'" With a biblical imagination in the poets' weight class, Sue hears God's word alive for this day: "You are the person" (2 Samuel 12), "Here am I, send me" (Isaiah 6), "Behold the Lamb of God" (John 1:29), "O God, you are my God!" (e.g., Psalm 63).

Sue is a long ponderer, deeply rooted in the Bible and a theology of the cross that announce how Jesus enters into human despair with free grace that creates hope, love, joy, and new life. For her, the question of *good anger* gains specificity relative to the biblical story, the person of Jesus, and realities of brokenness that slash people's abilities to live in their belovedness. She's dwelt deeply with her experiences of anger, use of anger in her work as a leader, critical evaluation of its roles in motivating struggles for social transformation, and perception of its detrimental and beneficial effects on whole communities. Jesus agitated her into leadership that mattered for marginalized communities, and she suspects the living God may just agitate others—that is, see them fully, call them boldly to be all they are, and set them in the midst of God's mission. She trusts that in every new age, God draws leaders into the pulpits and parks and paths and protests where God dwells mightily for the life of the world.

CHAPTER EIGHT

Feeling, Thinking, and Acting Splendidly

Virtuous Living and Agapic Anger

Cultivating virtue around a type of anger inflected with love, hope, and courage is important. It is virtue ethics that reveals how to cultivate that good habit. Broadly speaking, virtue ethics is about feeling, deliberating, and acting well for the flourishing of all living things. There are ways people can move more fully into their own virtue and flourishing and coach others toward the same faithful freedom.

CULTIVATING STABLE HABITS

Virtue ethics is an approach to ethics that concerns what it is to feel, move, and act well. *Well*, in this instance, means in a manner consistent with the good, where *the good* is shared human flourishing. Flourishing should not be confused with a life of ease; it is more about having come alive. People can attain a measure of flourishing while juggling persistent pressures such as resisting systemic injustices, cultivating relationships of depth, drawing people toward actualizing their own potential, selecting focused issues within the cacophony of massive societal woes, receiving flak for challenging comfortably powerful people and systems, or running sometimes dicey actions to bring about change that benefits vulnerable populations. Yet, flourishing is possible, and flourishing feels good. Still, flourishing won't turn human lives into places of ease and pure comfort.

Flourishing is not simple, partially because cultivating virtues is itself effortful. That is because virtues refer to stable habits that orient a person toward the good and allow her to be well and do well, and one acquires a virtue through habituation; it takes time and iterative practice to develop desired habits. Consider an imperfect analogy. US Women's National Team and Chicago Fire goalkeeper Alyssa Naeher's clutch save of a penalty kick preserved the lead in the 2019 World Cup semifinal. In an instant, Naeher responded to intercept the ball that the striker had drilled toward the goal's low corner. Through many hours of practice, she had increased her likelihood to respond well. After thousands of drills, games, misses, and saves, Naeher cultivated an instinctive tendency to move well in the goal area. An amateur or weekend athlete likely would respond differently while Naeher has habituated herself with excellence to the practices of a goalie.

Virtue ethics would say Naeher habituated herself to *skills*, which are usually distinguished from *virtues*. Skills can be applied in ways that either serve or detract from ethically valuable ends, whereas virtues, by definition, orient people toward what is honorable. A person could be a great goalie but a corrupt individual; similarly, one could be a terrible goalie but a good person. Although skills and virtues differ, there is a similarity between the process by which people become habituated to virtue and the process by which they acquire practical skills. "We become builders by building and lyre-players by playing the lyre. Similarly, we become just by doing what is just, temperate by doing what is temperate, and brave by doing brave deeds."[1] The soccer analogy illumines a *process* of habituation that is similar whether acquiring skills or forming good character. Naeher having conditioned herself to predictably choose well in the box is a skill, but character traits she's developed partially on the soccer field and through a similar iterative process of practice can be about virtue—things like being fair, caring for just outcomes like equal pay across the sport, and bravely facing world-class strikers flashing across the goal.

Virtuous habituation is a sort of identity formation by which one comes to predictably respond well. Responding well occurs on many intersecting planes—including emotion, thought, and action. In reality, these three are ever intertwined. For example, discernment may affirm and thus reinforce some emotions and actions. On the other hand, discernment may challenge and criticize other emotions and actions and, therefore, lead to them being discarded or modified. Everyone wobbles from time to time. When a response is inconsistent with values, a new decision can be made.

Virtuous habits are formed in communities with the help of mentors and through practice and reflection—not in isolation. Overt mentorship becomes less requisite when a person acquires virtues to such an extent that the "good" of a certain habit really has become characteristically hers. Yet, virtue is never on autopilot; rather, virtue must continuously be formed through lifelong practice. Naher's coach Paul DelloStritto coached her from the time she was thirteen through her college years. He trained her year after year toward excellence in her field. She says, "He believed in me from day one and was a huge piece of my journey."[2]

DelloStritto isn't her coach any longer. Mentorships can shift over time, becoming more mutual, akin to what philosophers call character friendship. Eventually, external mentorship is no longer as needful, although the need for community, practice, and reflection remains. Yet, even when one habitually internalizes virtues, community remains necessary in the form of relationships in which virtues are practiced and in the form of friendships in which a person actualizes her truest self.

Virtues are stable habits, yet habituation occurs through iterative practices, which may seem contradictory. Yet iterative design often creates the greatest stability. The meaning of "stability" in virtue ethics deserves some attention. Stability doesn't mean unchanging or constant in the sense that it is attained and then no longer requires cultivation; it is maintained only through continual cultivation. Aquinas says, "[A] habit of use is nothing else than a habit acquired by use."[3] "Stable" in virtue ethics means durable, lasting. Stability itself is a matter of ongoing renewal and depends on ongoing reconstitution that occurs through virtue-aligned practices. Habits of responding well to life situations can empower a person to move as though instinctively through situations of ethical import.

Practiced stability of virtues enables a person to deal well when new situations arise; circumstances can change, and a person's capacity to deal with change can evolve as well. The understanding of virtuous behavior that a white lad in the United States had in the 1950s is different from the conception of virtuous behavior that the same man has access to in 2025. In order for him to exhibit durable, stable habits of virtue, he actually would have to discard certain distorted views of gender roles, for example, and replace them with now-accessible insights regarding gender equity.

Over time, as awareness and capacities change, virtues evolve. The goal remains human flourishing across communities, but what this means to various people changes, partly through ongoing critical thought and debate. Human views and habits are culturally and historically contingent and can become disordered if they are not updated as times change. Virtue formation is a continual endeavor that ever inspires and exceeds one's quest for formation.

People practice into virtue—that is, they work to establish stable habits that dispose them to receive, perceive, and respond well in disparate situations. The central habit considered in these pages is that of responding to relevant situations with virtuous anger. A virtue ethics approach is flexible enough to acknowledge that anger appears in a lot of different guises. Kelly, Mary, Drea, and Sue deem good the anger to which they assent because it helps them recognize injustice, access courage, and bring about social transformation. The formation of good habits of being moved by ethically salient perceptions, such as perceptions of injustice, is crucial for living a Christian life.

FEELING, THINKING, AND ACTING WELL

Three general movements of virtue ethics include feeling, deliberating, and acting well. While most people will find one of these three harder than the others, it is possible to anger well in regard to all three. These movements work together with fluidity. To some extent it is artificial to separate them. Nevertheless, it is helpful to distinguish them in order to show that virtue is not simply about doing the right thing. It is also about how one perceives the world. It is about feeling emotions in ways that reflect good judgments about the world and deliberating with communal good in mind.

The women's well-honed strategies reflect the fact that they prioritize emotionally conscious, thought-filled action. Drea says, "I think anger is what's going to get the country to actually change. We have a whole bunch of angry people right now in our country, right? So many angry people. But I'd see the way of changing is to get them action-oriented. 'Oh, you're mad at [politician X]? Why don't you go and register 100 people to vote?' You have to pivot their anger towards solution. I think you need some good people—some good organizers, some good strategists, some people that are okay with listening and being okay with anger. You gotta be okay with it."

"Oh, you're angry; let me listen."

"You're angry; now what?"

"You're angry at the Board President for X, Y and Z. Alright; well, maybe we should get a meeting with him. Here's our talking points. Here's our ask."

"Oh, that didn't work? Now we need to go to their boss, or their funders."

"You can do a lot with anger; you just have to be able to organize it." Although Drea and others move toward action, they recognize that any action that is informed by virtuous anger will include wisdom in the pursuit of justice. Neighbor-edifying action flows from feeling and reflecting well in relation to anger. In other words, when you sense anger and add deliberation, you get to choose commendable ways to act.

EMOTIONS THAT TELL THE TRUTH

Many people think of emotions as happenings over which they have little if any control, but it is possible to transform the way in which anger works so that it can motivate needed change. This requires working with one's anger so it tends predictably away from suffering and toward the good they love. By assenting to agapic anger, one chooses to love justice, to hope for the world as it could be, and to enact courage to face arduous challenges. In the midst of all that effort, people can remain happy, oriented toward communal flourishing, and connected to good people.

Such cultivation is possible, in part, because emotions are complex processes that influence and can also be influenced by the people who undergo them. So, emotions both do and don't just happen. They do just spring up in the sense that they arise whether one wants them or not, whether convenient or not, and whether perfectly congruent with cognition or not. There remains a reflex-quality to some segments of emotion. On the other hand, emotions don't just happen in the sense that there is nothing people can do about them. Humans can shape how they feel to some extent.

Because of our phenomenal ability to be reflexive and practice integrating behaviors, people can begin to feel emotions in ways more adaptable to their own and their communities' flourishing. This certainly can go the other way too, and people can come to feel emotions in ways that hurt them or limit their life prospects. Remember Sue describing how, as a child, she held several things at once: she wasn't supposed to act angry, she was rewarded for being a family peacemaker, and she got cared for when she cried. This suite of realities set her up to perceive her anger as sadness and required her to learn as an adult how to distinguish between the two.

Emotions, including anger, affect what world people notice and have a chance of building. Cates writes, "[An emotion] can affect our thoughts, perceptions, desires, judgments, deliberations, decisions, actions, and interactions."[4] With emotions potentially affecting so much of who people are, how they interpret the world, and how they respond to what they think has happened or could happen, it is extremely important to recognize that most people can reflect on and direct their emotions as they occur, thereby cultivating good habits of being moved. Emotions' capacity to bear on decision making is crucial to Aristotle, who writes that "every virtue or excellence both brings into good condition the thing of which it is the excellence and makes the work of that thing be done well."[5] Agapic anger disposes people to perceive the belovedness of God's good creation enough that they notice when it's harmed, and to be energized to act justly for its well-being.

Some have said that anger is not possible to do well. Roman Stoic philosopher Seneca says anger is a "desire to inflict punishment."[6] He understands it as "a short madness: for it is equally devoid of self-control, regardless of decorum, forgetful of kinship, obstinately engrossed in whatever it begins to do, deaf to reason and advice, excited by trifling causes, awkward at perceiving what is true and just, and very like a falling rock which breaks itself to pieces upon the very thing which it crushes."[7] On his view, the emotion of anger is precisely a loss of the ability to reason and make reasonable choices, so it is not surprising that Seneca does not believe it is possible to rationally guide one's anger while one is feeling it.

Aristotle, on the other hand, says, "Let us then define anger as a longing, accompanied by pain, for a real or apparent revenge for a real or apparent slight, affecting a [wo]man [her]self or one of [her] friends, when such a slight is undeserved."[8] On his view, the power to reason is not necessarily undone by a bout of anger, and emotions can be more or less informed by good thinking. By implication, virtuous anger is possible. "The man who is angry at what he should be and with whom he should be, and, further, as he should, when he should, and for as long as he should, is praised. For the good-tempered man tends . . . to be angry in the manner, at the things, and for the length of time, that reason dictates."[9] Today one might hear, "This is neither the time nor the place to be angry," which implies an ability to examine and check one's own anger. Certain boundaries delineate what counts as praiseworthy anger; generally speaking, most people have at least some power to observe those boundaries, especially when they claim this power and practice into it. It is possible to perceive anger in a way that contributes to our own flourishing, find expression in actions that benefit others, and make it easier over time to get anger right in a wide range of circumstances, some of which cannot be predicted ahead of time.

INCREASING AGENCY THROUGH THOUGHTFULNESS

People can choose to feel anger without simply becoming consumed by it. Through the following six-step path that takes its inspiration from Aquinas, one can come to predictably deliberate well while negotiating initial emotions and moving toward action. This is how to cool anger well.[10] The path moves through the steps of noticing what is happening, taking counsel, and making solid choices. Next, it moves through consenting to what you've chosen, resolving to act, and doing it.

First, notice what is happening inside. Once aware of some anger, notice what harm the anger is reacting against as well as what good could be present (instead of the harm). Next, take counsel by asking the questions that help unearth the information you need to move into a decision-making phase. People can often initially counsel themselves by figuring out if assenting to this anger is praiseworthy. Angers worth assenting to meet certain criteria: the value violation is right to be angry about, it is yours to be angry about, the intensity of anger is right-sized to the violation, the timing of a response is appropriate, achieving good relative to the value violation is likely, and communities benefit. Two guardrails exist: acting upon initial incendiary bursts of anger is rarely virtuous; instead, work with initial flares of anger until they are cooled and take on a prosocial focus. Additionally, agapic anger does not nurture the goal of paying back an offender; while moving away from sources of harm, the goal of agapic anger is love-inflected. After counseling oneself, it may be helpful to externally process with one of the wise people in one's life who has steered you right in the past or whose perspective helps you ask more expansive questions.

The third step is to make a good choice about how you want to behave. Most people need to eliminate the pressure to make the perfect choice as perfection is not a rational quality for humanity and perfection is so often the enemy of good. Make a good decision; then, if later a more advisable path emerges, make a new good decision. To make the best possible decisions, continue blending reason with one's anger. Reason considers things such as how safe it is to address the harm, what resources and support are needed to address this healthfully, for whom will addressing it do good and does that person agree, whether this response is consistent with the best of who you are, and what the likely repercussions of this choice are.

Then move on to consenting to what has been chosen. In this long-pondering process, a decision does not immediately mean action; rather, a decision provides the conditions necessary to assent to it. Approve and embrace the choice. Should assenting not be possible to wisely give, then, revisit the previous steps. This is a stage to notice how the decision is sitting with you. Places of unease are taken seriously and addressed as potential sites of wisdom. Be able to articulate to another why you assent to this choice. Notice whose support is needed and wanted, and talk to them. Finally, do the research, coalition building, and planning that is required.

In the fifth step, one resolves to act. Ground in to the resilience needed for this action and settle one's body. Notice what it might take for one's whole body to feel congruent with this action. Assessing one's level of readiness may surface more things that are helpful to work through, while remembering that some people will feel itching to act the whole time and others might feel they would never be completely ready.

Up to this point there are fairly clear exit ramps to take when one finds that acting on this anger is not virtuous or not currently within one's bandwidth for doing this healthfully. The final step is to act. The decision and plan you made, researched, and pondered gets enacted in the world. Action also gets reflected on by considering what's going well, what needs adjusting, how leaders are faring, and whether this is having its intended impact. Even in the action step, modifications remain possible as more information emerges.

While working through these steps, the women exclude most forms of anger, so it is unsurprising that many of the initial angers brought to this process don't make it through the whole way—at least not in the form in which they entered. Cultivating dispositions that help people regularly perceive accurately and act well (being neither excessively nor deficiently angry, for example, and expressing anger in constructive ways) requires *phronesis*—a practical wisdom which enables people to feel and act on an emotion like anger without compromising their integrity. Anger does not have to morally compromise a person. Rather, a well-conditioned moral *imaginaire* and the cultivation of praiseworthy dispositions can develop through intentional interanimated processes of being moved and moving oneself well into action in ways that express practical wisdom.

The women can choose to feel and work with their own and other's anger without anger becoming a consuming force in their lives or causing them to lash out in unproductive ways because thought and practical wisdom condition their work with anger. Their process of being moved and helping others move well in relation to wisely formed anger is partially constitutive of their happiness (eudaimonistic flourishing). They are disposed to love justice and act for the transformation needed by vulnerable communities. From the perspective of the women's stories, conditioning anger—especially by love, hope, and courage—enables them to be emotionally clear, focused, and flexible; it enables them to be buoyed by anger, rather than losing themselves to it.

VALUE-ALIGNED ACTIONS

Anger can be enacted in ways consistent with virtue ethics, but it takes this good combination: a virtuous blend of being moved well in relation to anger and moving oneself to choose well. Aquinas says, "Human virtue which is an operative habit, is a good habit, productive of good works."[11] Even virtues that are about emotion are ultimately action-oriented because virtues are operative—they do things. Emotions can awaken one to what's real, mingle with wisdom, and motivate collective action. In the case of a justice-oriented anger, those actions are going to take the form of public actions that benefit the whole.

Human action is a constituent part of what it means to be human—to be created *imago Dei*. Action, then, is not a mere consideration in virtue ethics but is an inception and foundation of ethics. Cates also highlights the importance of action in Thomistic virtue ethics. "Aquinas's theory of action . . . distinguishes between interior acts and outward or outwardly visible acts, behaviors, or expressions. It shows how interior acts are typically continuous with patterns of outward behavior."[12] It is the end desired—the effect—that orients the whole process of decision making, and very often, the end desired is a state of affairs that can be brought about only through deliberate action.

Aquinas, who sees virtues as vital to a person's actions in community, provides four criteria for assessing good versus bad action.[13] Although he is focused on individual action, I, aware of his view that the common good supersedes individual good, take his criteria as transferable to the communal level. These criteria can help assess the ethical value of action: end, place, circumstance, and intensity/duration.[14] For each criteria, an example of setting explosives well is provided. Although that is a skill rather than a virtue, it nevertheless provides insight into a virtue ethics evaluation of actions.

- **End: How good is the goal at which the action aims?** The ethicality of setting an explosion to harm people's lives differs vastly from the value of setting an explosion in order to save people trapped behind rubble. An action attains to some measure of goodness on account of the end goal being good.
- **Place: How fitting is the location of the action?** Even if she sets just the right-sized explosion for the job, carrying it out in the wrong spot could be disastrous. For her action to be appropriate, as well as skillful, all relevant details of the context are considered with care.
- **Circumstance: How well or poorly does the situation fit the action?** Setting a blast without the official permit would display a lack of skill—for the end desired could be disrupted by legal action. Setting a blast in earshot of people who have suffered trauma from previous explosions could trigger people. Fit requires the assessment of any number of factors—for example, timing, legality, or cultural considerations. An action could be virtuous given one set of circumstances, and the same action could be vicious in another situation. This raises more questions, such as how far to go to understand potential impacts on people who may be affected, and how communication needs to happen.
- **Intensity/Duration: How appropriate is the action's potency?** Consider that a person setting either too big or too small of an explosion could turn out poorly. In ethical terms, setting an explosion

that is too big could injure bystanders unnecessarily; setting one that is too small could cost precious time in a rescue mission.

It is worth noting that while Aquinas does provide these four criteria for assessing the goodness of any given action, he does not presume that these four criteria are sufficient for determining the full ethicality of every action. He recognizes that the goodness of something remains a relative judgment situated among scores of factors that together contribute to what *all* is at stake.

These multiple ways the goodness of an action is gauged reveal that any given action can be more or less thoroughly good. "Nothing hinders an action that is good in one of the ways mentioned above, from lacking goodness in another way," says Aquinas.[15]

Furthermore, far more flexibility and nuance are required than may first be apparent upon reading the criteria. To start with, not all four of the criteria may be equally germane in any given case. The four criteria and interpretations of them are always being adapted to new or especially complicated situations. In addition, a high degree of subjectivity remains even as a person uses some criteria to assess an event. While criteria are helpful, they can be problematic when not used with flexibility and reflexivity.

Still, enacting anger has some bearing on just social action. In pursuit of social transformation, the women both wield anger themselves and help others fare well with anger that meets distinct standards. Agapic anger, for the organizers and religious leaders, is grounded in the love of justice, in which both emotion and volition are involved. Just social action aims at creating conditions that facilitate the active enjoyment of good by the most people possible, especially benefiting publics in need. Thus, just social action will not primarily benefit the self or a privileged subset of a population. Because there are many ways for enacted anger to miss a virtuous mark, these women assess the value of action through what they refer to as "impact" over "intention." *Intending* good is necessary but is not enough. It matters to Drea, Sue, Kelly, and Mary that people concern themselves with effecting a good *impact*, whether that means material change in the distribution of power or changes in people's character, and so on.

Finally, *just social action* must be tangible. Although it might be apparent that enactment is part of action, the clarification made here is that actions such as deliberating internally, persuading oneself, or even changing one's heart do not yet cut muster to be called just social action. Although silent, internal, and private actions are foundational to just social action, just social action is not reducible to internal movements. An individual tends to be capable of just social action as an extension of virtuous interior acts.

Public enactment of virtue moves beyond the private or personal and takes place in publics. Its value is not just that it occurs in publics but also that it serves publics. A person's just action that benefits a wider community could go unobserved, yet still be just social action. A virtue ethic of just social action generates a productive topography for considering community organizers' efforts to form and actively employ agapic anger for the sake of justice-advancing action. People can be formed with the virtue of justice-seeking. It comes about by repeatedly choosing well how to regard and treat one's fellow human beings. A person attains virtue by practicing into it in a community whose flourishing she values.

Cultivating a good habit of experiencing anger and tapping into it deliberately for a purpose is possible because of fluid and collaborative movements among people's responses to what is sensed, their ability to talk themselves into how to act, and their power to act. Separated out into the movements of feeling, deliberating, and acting, this is what is happening: on the level of sensing, people move toward what they perceive as suitable and away from what they perceive as harmful. On the level of volition, people think, deliberate, and make choices in relation to their emotions. This allows people to consciously form habits of being well moved by those emotions. On the level of external movement, people can let the first two (feeling well and deliberating well) inform their actions. If they do, the action could be viewed as being motivated, in part, by reflective emotion—a thought-filled anger.

ASSESSING THE GOODNESS OF AGAPIC ANGER

The work of Thomas Aquinas has helped not only to articulate and analyze the process of agapic anger as it is choreographed, but also to evaluate it—or particular examples of it—ethically. Recall that Aquinas specifies four criteria whereby a given moral act can be evaluated ethically, which I state as five questions.

- How good is the **end** at which the action aims?
- How fitting is the **place** of the action?

- How well or poorly does the **circumstance** accommodate the action?
- How appropriate is the action's **intensity** and/or **duration**?
- How good is the **end** at which choreographies of agapic anger aim?

The women specifically help people turn their anger away from individualized recipients or from forms such as payback. These goals (individualizing and paying back) register with the women as counterproductive, not only for the success of their specific social actions, but also to their own moral development. First, investing oneself in a desire that some individual might change his poor behavior or way of thinking misses a crucial tenet of organizing, namely that a whole system created an individual to have the capacity or privilege to behave poorly so the whole system needs to be addressed. When a whole system changes, the potential for more people to flourish may significantly increase. One characteristic of agapic anger, then, is that it is deliberately calibrated toward the causes of widespread suffering and the promotion of the social good. For example, on Sue's view, anger at patriarchal constraints of herself and other women would be less productively spent on individuals because so little real change for society comes about by being angry with one person. Instead of spending her energy on singular occurrences of injustice, Sue chooses to expend it where and when she deems it will make a lasting, structural difference.

Second, aiming to pay someone back for his slight is unreasonable because what was lost from the violation is not recoverable. Mary tells a story about her dad's premature death on account of toxic exposures at the steel company. Mary does not try to pay the steel company back—they cannot restore her father to her. Mary, instead, looks for what pays off. Instead of payback, organizers want the energy of their anger to pay off in the currency of greater moral goodness for the lives of many people. Inasmuch as the women help people connect their anger to what they love, calibrate it to communal/political levels, and orient it toward justice, they give expression to virtue and further cultivate virtue.

The *places* where choreographies of agapic anger occur are fitting. In terms of virtue ethics, one might think of "place" in terms of context.[16] What is the context in which work on agapic anger occurs, and how fitting is that context? Transforming anger occurs in the context of deliberate, public relationships. Virtue is developed in relationships with mentors, friends, and wider publics, but most notably with people who are in the deliberate pursuit of goodness.

Early on in processes of moral formation, people need mentors such as these women. After practicing repeatedly, peer friendships can suffice to maintain the virtue. Transforming anger is a process of moral formation. It is ill-advised to experience or express anger alone because it takes a community to anger well. Choreographies of agapic anger take up residence in purposefully cultivated, fitting, and virtuous relationships, regardless of precise location.

Agapic anger is appropriate to the **circumstances** the women address. Circumstances are multifactorial, and there is no way to address the circumstances of multiple leaders working on different projects with Mary in Chicago, Berkeley, San Diego, and so on; Drea in Chicago; Sue in Minneapolis; and Kelly in Palmer, Alaska. The focus here is on a particularly crucial element of the circumstance of agapic anger, namely, the gap between the "world as it is" and "world as it should be." For example, in the world as it is, Drea attests to several girls living on the south side of Chicago without the presence of their deported fathers. If that is the world as it is, then what is the world as the women's faith values would have things be?

Sue's Lutheran denomination composed an official social statement on immigration that says,

> The leaders and congregations that have given us this legacy [of hospitality for refugees] remind us that hospitality for the uprooted is a way to live out the biblical call to love the neighbor in response to God's love in Jesus Christ. They recall for us God's command to Israel: "The stranger who resides with you shall be to you as the citizen among you; you shall love the stranger as yourself, for you were strangers in the land of Egypt: I am the Lord your God" (Leviticus 19:34). They direct us to where Jesus said he is present: "I was a stranger and you welcomed me" (Matthew 25: 35). They call on Martin Luther to ask us: "How do we know that the love of God dwells in us? If we take upon ourselves the need of the neighbor." Our desire is to carry on their faith and practice, their exemplary way of faith being active in love.[17]

Sue's denomination states a vision of the world as it could be where hospitality for refugees is the norm. The Lutheran Church provides this ethical model; Scripture demands noncitizens be treated as justly as citizens, and God's presence stirs people to act in love on behalf of the neighbor.

Mary, in Roman Catholic practice, might look to the US Conference of Bishops' statement, "Welcoming the Stranger among Us: Unity in Diversity," which states, "Both the Old and New Testaments tell compelling stories of refugees forced to flee because of oppression. . . . With God's powerful intervention [the Israelites] were able to escape and take refuge in the desert. For forty years they lived as wanderers with no homeland of their own."[18] The bishops claim refugee status as an important part of Roman Catholic religious heritage. Their statement then identifies three main principles regarding immigration: people have the right to immigrate, countries have the right to regulate their borders, and countries need to carry out border regulation with justice and mercy.[19] In the explanation of the third principle, the bishops elaborate:

> The Catholic Church teaches that every person has basic human rights and is entitled to have basic human needs met. . . . Undocumented persons are particularly vulnerable to exploitation. . . . Current immigration policy that criminalizes the mere attempt to immigrate and imprisons immigrants who have committed no crime or who have already served a just sentence for a crime is immoral.[20]

The Roman Catholic statement purports that in the world as it should be, countries treat people who migrate or immigrate with justice and mercy by providing for basic needs and protecting those who are vulnerable from exploitation, criminalization, and paying more than a just amount for an offense.

Kelly, a deaconess in the United Methodist Church (UMC), could look to her denomination's Church and Society statement that offers a biblical frame, again citing the Leviticus and Matthew scriptures, as did the Lutheran and Catholic churches. This statement also points to Jesus's own refugee status and a text from the book of Hebrews that "tells us that in opening our homes to guests, we may be 'entertaining angels without knowing it.'" The UMC statement says, "US policy has focused on enforcement, rather than addressing root causes."[21] The statement calls UMC congregations to address causal issues with specific actions, including to:[22]

- encourage legislation that supports the rights of migrants and provides pathways to legal status;
- resist racism, xenophobia, and violence against migrants and, instead, build relationships;
- denounce a wall between the United States and Mexico;
- demand the US government to stop arresting, detaining, and deporting undocumented immigrants until an immigration reform policy is in place.

The UMC statement concludes by providing resources and offering specific ideas of what individuals can do.

All three statements[23]—the Lutheran, Roman Catholic, and Methodist— regard two shared biblical texts as foundational to their reasoning, namely Leviticus 19, which identifies hearers with those who have been strangers and exhorts hearers to treat strangers as citizens, and Matthew 25, where Jesus— redeemer and life-giver in Christian religious belief—himself identifies as a stranger and blesses those who welcomed a stranger, unaware that they were welcoming him. As these thrice-affirmed biblical texts declare, the world as it should be identifies with those who find themselves vulnerable regarding their status of citizenship and changes due to immigrants' presence and excellence.

Mary thinks that values formed by Christian faith make a difference in a person's daily actions. She might say that a faith that is not consistently put into action is hard to recognize as faith. "So, if you really have a set of values and a faith tradition that's important to you, then you say, 'How am I going to make this real? Real in the real world? Not in heaven, but right here?'" The world-as-it-could-be, which is evidenced in the official statements above, stands in contrast to the world-as-it-is that reinforces systems of domination and oppression. The women find such gaps disquieting and choose to defy the pressure to maintain or be silent about such gaps. For these women, the world affirmed by their faith values is indeed a world worth pursuing and a world that reasonably can be more actualized. While there is pain in more proficiently recognizing these gaps, the women do not act to avoid pain. Rather, they choose to be attuned to the pain of others and experience pain because of their hope. As Kelly has said, it is hope that moves people who can see the world-as-it-could-be to action. She is clear: "You can't have the hope unless at the core you know that there is a behavior that is happening, and it can be changed." Particular circumstances of life-threatening gaps between the world-as-it-is and the world-as-it-could-be lend themselves well to the cultivation and practice of virtuous anger.

Agapic anger's *intensity* and *duration* are appropriate to the work of community organizing. Aquinas holds that actions and emotions need to be of suitable intensity and duration. Anger just is an intense emotion, as charting its activation of the frontal cortex displays. The women take it to be true that people who care about justice and injustice are already exposed to the intense emotion of anger. Even the rather strong intensity of the organizers' and leaders' anger can be virtuous. Aquinas, following Aristotle, understands "gentleness" as anger's mean, that is, the center between a blameworthy lack of anger and a blameworthy excess of anger. The concept of gentleness could seem incongruous with anger, but not finding a better word, Aristotle says, "[A person] may then be called gentle-tempered . . . who feels anger on the right grounds and against the right persons, and also in the right manner and at the right moment and for the right length of time."[24]

The organizers' anger can be considered gentle in this sense. As the women work anger from raw into agapic forms, their anger does achieve a "gentleness" of sorts when it addresses fitting causes and people and if its manner, moment, and duration is likewise apt. If anger is intense, it can be rightly intense, given the size of the structural offense with which the women are dealing.

However, the term "gentleness" is itself problematic today and needs to be rethought. The problem is that women in the United States have been culturally conditioned to enact a certain form of gentleness that has impeded women's leadership. "Cross-national research on gender stereotypes reports that women are consistently perceived as possessing traits such as kindness, cooperation, compassion, warmth, and gentleness; whereas men are viewed to be more aggressive, firm, authoritative, and powerful."[25] But the quality of gentleness is "often regarded as less valuable to leadership in the US culture than are males' socially accepted agentic, demanding, and delegation-based leadership."[26] The word "gentleness" has lost, in contemporary society, some of its value in describing virtues. Revised language is needed for this cognition-inflected, communally minded anger. Today, "justice-attuned anger" better describes anger done well than does gentleness.

The women sustain a long *duration* of anger that is fitting for their trans-formative choreography. Aquinas viewed anger as short-lived except when the anger-producing stimulus is repeatedly present. Determining the "right" duration of anger under either circumstance is a matter of judgment. The women recognize that serious injustices are persistently present. One can argue, therefore, that the anger they cultivate in their work appropriately has a long duration. The duration is rightly as long as their anger serves to constitute and further motivate ongoing transformation.

Mary retells and relives painful stories that extend the duration of her vital connection to her anger "because I've got to be reminded that there's shit in this world." As an act of love, she stirs in herself the memory of a particular injustice to which she is bodily and palpably connected in order to stay alive and attuned to other real injustices because she believes people need motivating energy to persist in pursuits of justice. Mary repeatedly exposes herself to the pain of the negative because she believes it is a crucial part of sustaining her love of justice. Agapic anger's long duration does not, in and of itself, undermine its moral goodness. It does not cause the women to become angry people, but rather increases their freedom and flourishing.

After presenting examples of both quickly finished and long-held anger, Aquinas discusses his moral evaluation of anger. Anger is blameworthy to the extent that it hinders the use of cognition—a moral difficulty Aquinas thinks regularly occurred with anger.[27] Clear thinking is required to attain to consistently right action. Agapic anger is blended with wise cognition. Increased blending of anger with rational thought potentiates increased clarity of moral reasoning. Therefore, it can indeed be morally responsible to endorse agapic anger and teach others to do the same.

In terms of the end, circumstance, place, and intensity/duration, the moral value of both transforming anger and pursuing social change compatible with agapic anger can make these actions praiseworthy. Just because the organizers' choreographies of agapic anger are commendable does not mean that the women rest assured that such processes will inevitably yield the good. They remain vigilant when working with anger because they are aware of the many ways and moments anger can veer from virtuous paths in either obvious or occluded ways. With caution ever present, enactments of agapic anger in publics can serve to shape resilient leaders and increase the potency of social transformation efforts. Therefore, with reference to the main tradition of virtue ethics in the Western world, one can deem it ethically responsible and even required to get angry with perceived injustices that really *are* contrary to human well-being.

CHAPTER NINE

Practiced Wisdom

Structural Implications of Agapic Anger

Current postcolonial, womanist, and Queer theories identify structural implications that often had been overlooked in classical philosophy. Tools like structural power analyses and consideration of a politics of privilege can critique and extend Aristotelian and Thomistic philosophies of anger and virtue ethics. The following three structural moves add decolonial and antiracist lenses needed to think better about the needs for, approach to, and value of agapic anger.

MOVING FROM INDIVIDUALS TO SYSTEMS

Male philosophers from antiquity and the medieval era thought that people's anger was mostly a response to individual abusers. Aristotle says, "If this definition [of anger] is correct, the angry man must always be angry with a particular individual (for instance, with Cleon, but not with men generally) and because this individual has done, or was on the point of doing, something against him or one of his friends."[1] Aquinas says similarly that anger "ensues from someone having injured us by his action. Now all actions are the deeds of individuals: and consequently, anger is always pointed at an individual."[2]

The women's practical wisdom challenges the tradition from Aristotle to Aquinas and beyond. The organizers see that abusive systems also cause anger. In their professional roles, they find anger that is pointed only at an individual abuser to be morally suspect, minimally effective, and, therefore, off-target and wasteful of their anger energy. The women see clearly that anger needs to be able to be directed at harmful structures, institutions, and systems.

Drea says, "So, anger brought me to the movement" of professional community organizing. "Some of my life experiences of poverty, injustice, racism—they all made me angry growing up, but I didn't know how to funnel that." What angers Drea is "poverty, injustice, racism." The systemic causes of her anger outstrip the individual causes that Aristotle and Aquinas envision. Aligning with Drea's perspective on systemic causes of anger, Kelly names the misuse of power, negligence, and sexism. Sue, too, diverges from Aristotle and Aquinas when she calls attention to patriarchy.

Pamela moves with ease from her anger at personal injury to anger at related communal injustices that damage whole swaths of people. "So, my story is about a lot of abandonment—about not being able to trust people in my life. . . . And when I see that out in the world, it makes me infuriated. There's lots of whole communities that we abandoned." She continues her story. "You know, I grew up outside of Detroit. . . . My mother used to call me a little old lady—I was such a serious child. But it was because I had so much responsibility. She was making suicide attempts once a year. She would disappear for weeks at a time, and you would come home from school, and you wouldn't know where she was or why there was a babysitter there."

"And then my dad was gone a lot and then [completed] suicide. There was just abandonment all over the place. And I think I knew as a kid, this is not what my life is supposed to be like. I'm not supposed to have this much responsibility or have to figure things out with my sister, with some babysitter who I've never met. You know? I'm eight years old, not knowing when my mother's going to come home, nobody telling you anything about where people are or what's going on. You get the sense, 'I am *wholly* alone.' And it was so unnecessary.

"It was so much a product of white culture and male culture and adultism, where you can't tell the kids what's going on. I got into therapy, and I was mad at my dad and at my mom—I went through that like individual level, but it's not hard to politicize it. My dad got dumped by a corporation that he worked for for thirty-five years. He had a reason to be depressed, right? It's not hard to politicize it. And then when you hear [others' stories]—like all of us have hundreds and hundreds of people's stories in our hearts, right? Hundreds of stories. Oh, those stories! So, tap into [them]!"

"People are put into prison and are working for twenty-five cents an hour. You just feel like they are truly alone. Who the heck's watching out for them?

How do they possibly organize any power? Or immigrants—they come here and then there's this narrative about immigrants—you know that they're taking [from] the system. Meanwhile they're paying taxes that they're never going to see benefits from. You know, they're making sure we can afford our vegetables and our fruits. The narrative is upside down about immigrants. It is fuckin' upside down."

> *Mary:* That's very intentional too.
> *Pamela:* Yea! And you just feel like people are alone—like as a collective—they're alone in their struggle.
> *Mary:* Just like you were.
> *Pamela:* Yep. Just like I was. And then white people are on the sidelines, "Well I can't get involved because it's not my issue or because I don't want to take over . . ." But fuck that. Bullshit. When someone says that in training, then that's when I'm like . . .
> *Sue:* Then you're mad—really in touch with your anger.
> *Pamela:* Yeah. I get really clear, "How dare you let yourself off the hook under some rubric of liberal appropriateness." Bullshit. And it's just all these kids—I [work with] a kid who's twenty years old, who's in his last year of college, who's going to have shitloads of student debt—even though he went to the state university, even though we're helping him. He's still gonna have debt. And then all the students I work with at People's Action—so my kid's gonna have like what $20,000 student debt—I work with kids who have like $60,000.
> *Mary:* How about $120,000?
> *Drea:* 80.
> *Pamela:* Yep. We're just like sending them out in sinking ships by themselves. How are they supposed to deal with that? Why aren't we collectively helping them? Like this is the fuckin' future and we're . . .
> *Drea:* Setting them up.
> *Sue:* Right. At best we're wringing our hands.
> *Pamela:* We're kicking them in the shins.

Pamela moves deftly from the abandonment she knew as an eight-year-old to structural levels—corporations discontinuing practices of loyalty and abandoning workers after years of faithful employment; exploitation of the prison population's labor; compromising, false narratives told to undermine immigrants; an educational-degree-oriented society paired with strangulating levels of educational debt. Pamela says, "It's not hard to politicize it." It is not hard to move from understanding the pain of abandonment she experienced to understanding how wracking kids with debt abandons them systemically to poverty. There is real fluidity for the organizers between the personal and structural.

The women recognize multiple forms of anger in various life circumstances, so they respond by first getting clear about personal injuries. In many ways they honor past and present personal anger by taking it as valid enough to get clear about its causes and the harm and good it can do and by constructively putting the energy associated with it toward the end of just social transformation. After getting clear, they then recalibrate their focus to the communal level and set their sights on an injury, an obstacle, a cause that they view as unjustly constraining whole communities. The women form themselves to recognize their anger, to quickly comprehend that an individual perpetrator is only a cog in a system, and to assess the system as the vastly more problematic entity. They, then, feel anger toward a system even while their stories tie them to particular instantiations of wrongdoing.

Mary Gonzales urges trainees to know their stories well so they can conjure them up when needed. Particular instances of anger generate an energy that Pamela and others transfer to communal problems. Yes, there are individual instantiations that stoke anger, but the women elevate their agapic anger for communal benefit. Even anger they do not deem worthwhile to act out on (like anger toward their fathers' patriarchal patterns) is honored as it is folded into and supplies energy for their current efforts. Community organizers base their anger also in love and transform themselves so that angry energy from a personal injury is reallocated to some threat to the community and is deescalated in relation to the personal.

It is like the mathematics make more sense this way: They have noticed that anger that stays on the individual level eats the angry person up, makes her more isolated, gives her less credibility, and may or may not change the one abuser. In contrast, anger recalibrated toward an abusive system honors her and her anger by releasing it, connecting her with community, giving her more credibility, and changing many people's well-being by constraining an abusive system from continuing to harm.

Not only do the women calibrate their anger to address abusive systems, they also habituate themselves to feel less anger toward individual slights done to them. The organizers stay in touch with past anger that they can direct toward something of benefit to others partly because they try not to waste present anger on things that are mostly personal. Sue questions what good it even does to be angry with one person when that person is merely symptomatic of a whole system. "I have learned from organizing that we are all part of systems, so the behaviors that we exhibit are, in part, because of the systems that we've been a part of. So, as much as I disdain [an exploitative politician], I'm also of the camp that if we just get rid of him, we haven't gotten rid of the problem because A) there's a lot of other individuals who he's just giving license to, but B) there's a system that just has created those behaviors and attitudes. I understand why he is the asshole that he is because he's just part of a family system, part of a cultural system that has given him money and license to express himself the way he does and to stir up other people to listen to their worst interests."

Continuing to think about anger targeting individuals versus systems, Sue adds an even more personal story. "I could point to [my father] and say he's my oppressor—he's the embodiment of my oppressor—except I loved him dearly. He was also a wonderful dad, and so there's that dichotomy. I realize that he embodied a lot of patriarchy and other things, and so, in organizing, we sometimes talk about naming your oppressor, and then the best way to get even with your oppressor is not to hurt *them* but to dismantle the systems in which they were able to become your oppressor.

"*What good would it do* the world if I somehow could punish him for some of the things that happened in my life? A) He didn't intend them to be that way, even though he was behaving in those ways, but B) it would just be *one* person, but then it's just repeated all over the world—that kind of patriarchy. So, let's dismantle patriarchy, right? I've learned in community organizing that our oppressor is really a symbol of the system in which they oppress us." Sue argues that being angry with either this politician or her dad would do little good because their behaviors were created by cultural systems, which continue to produce generations of the same sorts of men. Desiring punishment of these individuals is a flawed solution because punishing them could possibly curb one symptom of a destructive system, but it would waste the energy needed to change the system itself.

While organizing around the issues most important to a community, the women are not always focusing on issues that are most important to them personally. This reality raises the question: Why would a person expose themselves to anger or use energy on something that is not happening directly to them? Although she has no current personal need for state-run nursing home care, Kelly supported St. Michaels when they noticed the home was not receiving the funding appropriately due them. Although she is not an Alaska Native, when the Catholic Native Ministry "identified that they would like to start their own nonprofit organization," she said, "If Alaska Native Elders want to build an organization for the Elders in the Mat-Su that serves the Mat-Su Alaska Native Community, then I'm gonna help them."

This perspective aligns with the following story of Thomas Aquinas, who says, "the motive of a man's anger is always something done against him,"[3] but an "adversary" whom he imagines prods him saying, "[O]ne may desire *vindicta* for things done against others. Therefore we are not always angry on account of something done against us."[4] Aquinas responds with increased flexibility: "Injury done by anyone does not affect a man unless *in some way* it be something done against him."[5] According to Aquinas, a person is not angered if not personally slighted unless one of two "as though" conditions is met. First, a person could identify intimately with another person who gets slighted—a close friend, a family member. It could be, Aquinas reasons, that a person identifies so closely with another person that it is *as though* they were unified. "If we are angry with those who harm others and [desire] *vindicta*, it is because those who are injured belong in some way to us: either by some kinship or by friendship, or at least because of the nature we have in common."[6] In this instance, because a person feels united with the other person, it is *as though* they themselves were slighted. Perhaps Kelly has built deep relationships with Indigenous people in the Mat-Su and with community members who need the nursing home to thrive and has come to experience kinship. Perhaps she readily sees in her own life a compelling analogue to the others' situations, and that enables her to make the connection.

A second condition is present when a person intimately and personally identifies with some thing or concept *as though* it were a part of her or it partly defines her. "When we take a very great interest in a thing, we look upon it as our own good; so that if anyone despise it, it seems *as though* we ourselves were despised and injured."[7] For this condition to come into effect, a person must identify so closely with a thing (e.g., accessibility) or a concept (e.g., the idea that the prison industrial complex unfairly targets Black men) that an intimate connection is formed such that, in these examples, if an adversary rejects accessibility updates for a building or people dismiss the idea that racism and imprisonment collaborate to harm people, then the person senses pain.

Kelly and many organizing colleagues identify deeply with the people and issues with which they work. This deep identification is a trait of love. Their iteratively gained, oft-practiced, and long-held *caritas* disposes them to love well—to love themselves, others, and God well. As organizers, they love justice, so their love is oriented toward larger communities and common good. They love both their habit of acting in ways that benefit the common good and the actions and effects of justice that potentiate increased communal flourishing.

The women are moved by their anger. Partially because they refuse to repress their anger, they are able to notice what their anger is repulsed by (in Pamela's case, abandonment) and what their anger tends toward (real, long-lasting security for herself, for others). They recalibrate their anger to encompass communal or structural causes and goals. To a certain extent their anger takes up structural *causes* that are related to a personal injury but move beyond the personal to the communal, but they definitely recalibrate their anger to tend toward structural *goals*.

Pamela does not choose for her anger to propel her toward some magical rectification of her father's death or the aggregation of abandonments in her youth. Instead, she chooses to turn what could be personal anger toward the structural level she deems responsible by realizing that the infidelity of US company culture sows depression; she doesn't need to blame her parents because she recognizes cultural systems that conspired to create the conditions for job loss, inconsistency, and depression. Pamela, by identifying through love with others who experience related pain, enacts concrete, communal, political steps toward alleviating systems that fetter students with debt. Being moved by anger, recognizing it and choosing well, and acting accordingly, Pamela forms herself well in relation to anger in the midst of unfair tragedy.

IMPACT OVER INTENT

Aquinas says that:

> Injury is done to another in three ways: namely, through ignorance, through passion, and through choice. Then, most of all, a man does an injustice, when he

does an injury from choice, on purpose, or from deliberate malice. . . . Wherefore we are most of all angry with those who, in our opinion, have hurt us on purpose. For if we think that someone has done us an injury through ignorance or through passion, either we are not angry with them at all, or very much less: since to do anything through ignorance or through passion takes away from the notion of injury.[8]

Aquinas believes that deliberately inflicted injuries generate the most anger in a reasonable person, whereas injuries inflicted on account of ignorance cause little to no anger.

Mary and Sue disagree. They think injuries inflicted due to ignorance can indeed be just as serious and worthy of their anger as deliberate injuries. They each recounted stirring episodes from their childhoods when their loving fathers—with whom they remained in mutual loving relationships throughout their lives—unintentionally inflicted injury through patriarchal bias.[9] Their fathers behaved as they did because they were part of a system that made women's inferiority appear natural and obvious. Much the same system injures billions of women each day. In a way, the issue is not their father's ignorance but the fact that so many men benefit from participating in a system that allows them to harm women with impunity, and also lulls them into being unaware of most of what they are doing, thinking that everything is normal.

The community organizers reason that certain injuries like poverty, patriarchy, and racial inequity, including microaggressions and microinsults, need to be denounced. These injuries are systemically perpetrated and inflict harm on whole communities; they are often perpetrated below levels of human consciousness. "In our society we expect those who are oppressed and marginalized to eat from the table of injustice with a smile on their face. To do otherwise is to appear beastly, ungrateful, or un-American."[10] The organizer's focus on systemic, sometimes ignorant, injuries differs in an interesting way from Aquinas's view.

In alignment with Mary and Sue, Kelly shares a story from her seminary studies: "Our professor asked us to read this book, *The Soul of HipHop*, which is written by an African American/Mexican American man and his experience growing up in the ghetto. . . . Anyway, she phrased the prompt like 'I know some of you will have had a really hard time with this material this week, but let's push through it anyway. What are some of the things you could learn from these people about this kind of evangelism? And what are some things we can learn from them?'

"The language was microaggressive, and it made me feel sick; it made me feel bad. So, I asked my husband, 'Use *your* eyes; you read this. I know I'm seeing something but what is it that I'm seeing—you know, *exactly*?' So, he was able to highlight the words where these microaggressions were happening, and cultural appropriations: saying, 'What can we take from *them* and use for *us*?'[11] That's what the assignment was. 'What can we take from these Black and brown people and their experience of poverty'—she didn't go into it—just very plainly, 'What can we take from them and use for us?' It was more subtle than that. It still *was* that."

Kelly recalls that her emotions influenced her as her professor's unintentional microaggressive prompt made her feel ill. She felt "in her gut" that this prompt moved her to anger. She processed it with her spouse in order to pinpoint what it was about the prompt that incensed her. "So, I was faced with, Okay, this makes me angry. So, in my gut I check in . . . this makes me angry. I'm in a seminary. I'm in an institution of higher learning where I am supposed to be learning how to *NOT* do this—right? Yet, here my professor is doing this and encouraging the mostly—there's me and one other person of color in the class—teaching all these white people how to go into the world and do this. This is giving them [a positive take on cultural appropriation]." She weighed the pros and cons of responding to the professor and decided to request conversation. "So, I said, 'Okay, I've got to write to her.' So, I wrote her an email. And I rewrote it, and I rewrote it, and I rewrote it. But, basically, I was just very clear, and I named what it was that I was seeing.

"Specifically. I said, 'I want to bring to your attention some concerns that I have about your prompt, and I would like to talk to you about it.' I said, 'There's some language in your prompt here and here, and this microaggressive language is really concerning to me.'" Anger alerted Kelly that something was wrong and gave her motivation to do something about it. Following her conversation with Kelly, this professor rewrote the prompt, ran it by Kelly, and resubmitted it to the class. Her act of respectful critique resulted not only in a changed prompt, but also in the professor seeing in a new way and running the prompt by Kelly, who gained status in the exchange.

Kelly recognizes that, in terms of her level of anger, it mattered little that this professor's microaggressions came out of ignorance. She said, "It doesn't matter if it was intentional or unintentional. The hurt is the same, so it creates the same anger." She added that it might be easier to forgive if the slight is unintentional, "but the anger isn't less."

Sue notices two distinct benefits to letting anger address unintentional injuries—one benefit to others and one benefit to herself. "Our anger can help reveal our collusion with a system. There are still men in my life who, unbeknownst to them, are unaware of their male privilege or even their misogyny. They grew up in this culture, so they're going to have some of these behaviors. So, I could get angry with them, and they could be like, 'Woah! That's not what I meant.' And I could say, 'That was the impact.'

"There're two things. It might unveil something that they weren't aware of and then they can change or choose to do differently. But secondly, I get a voice instead of just taking it. Even if they don't change, I've inserted agency. I've become more liberated because I was willing to call it out—not just standing for it or rolling over for it." Sue sees the modulation of certain forms of anger—maybe here a form of recognition-anger or protection-anger—into agapic anger as an opportunity for liberation. The person or system that is corrected has a chance to live better in the world, rising more fully to their excellence. In addition, Sue gets to live more fully into her own excellence.

Aquinas notices that being forgetful of someone "is a clear sign of slight esteem" and provokes anger because "this seems to show that he thinks little of [us]."[12] On Aquinas's worldview, "[I]t is evident that the more excellent a [wo]man is, the more unjust is a slight offered [her] in the matter in which [s]he excels."[13] Taken together it would seem that Aquinas believes that being forgetful of a prominent person is a more unjust slight than being forgetful of people less known.[14]

Respected-in-his time and privileged, Aquinas was not able to notice what Drea Hall sees on a daily basis. Being forgetful about the youth on the south side of Chicago with whom Drea works—children who are not deemed "prominent" by the city's typical modes of evaluation (political power, educational hierarchy, class status, etc.) is a greater slight than failing to recognize more "prominent" leaders.

Slighting a person already disadvantaged by inequitable societal structures is more problematic—despite the fact that it is, inexcusably, more socially acceptable—than slighting a privileged person. Ethicist Michael P. Jaycox says, "[T]he reality is that patterns of systemic oppression and privilege at the societal level make such habits [as de-centering white privilege] ethically necessary."[15] Habits that expose "unintended" slights must be cultivated in a society remaining willfully or passively ignorant of them. A society that accepts unintentional slights is not holding privileged groups accountable, which in turn leaves the slighted group with diminished recourse.

BUILDING ENDURANCE

Aquinas, thinking mostly of one individual slighting another—for example, one man striking another—reasons that anger, unlike hatred, tends to "soon die away."[16] He wrote that anger is strongest right when the slight occurs and diminishes as our memory is weakened by time. Research psychologists Baas, De Dreu, and Nijstad provide data for much the same thing, showing that "arousing states such as anger mobilize energy and lead to increased expenditure of resources."[17] Anger's high intensity depletes resources quickly, so it corresponds with a short duration.

However, Aquinas, using an analogy between anger and friendship, also shows that anger can linger or build if the cause of anger remains present. Aquinas reasons that "in the presence of a friend, the cause of friendship is continually being multiplied by time: wherefore the friendship increases: and the same would apply to anger, were its cause continually multiplied."[18] In the event that the cause of anger was "continually multiplied," anger, like friendship, could also be sustained and even increase.

The women's exposure to injustice is prolonged, and thus their exposure to anger is often prolonged. Even though the process of dismantling abusive systems and achieving justice will take a long time to realize or may never be fully realized, still Sue, Kelly, Mary, and Drea still deem the pain of their work to be worth carrying. Professor and researcher in ethics, moral psychology, and feminist philosophy Lisa Tessman argues that the pain involved in seeking greater justice is not only worth enduring; it is an integral part of the process of responding well to human suffering.

> Because the absence of any pained response to another's suffering is so appalling, a program of engaging politically in social justice struggles without sensitivity and attention to the suffering one aims to end is unacceptable. This is unfortunate because political struggles not burdened with this disposition could perhaps proceed faster and more efficiently, free from the weight of anguish and less prone to consequent feelings of discouragement or hopelessness.[19]

One way to bear up successfully under this grief is by adding the energy from being appalled to the anger-energy. Tessman continues, "If sensitivity and attention to others' suffering does not do the work—at least not reliably—of compelling people to undertake social justice struggles, something else must provide this motivation: it could be a principled commitment to justice, perhaps in combination with other political emotions such as anger."[20] If it is unacceptable, as Tessman says, to be unaffected by people's struggles, then repeated or prolonged exposures to anger can be part of the life of church leaders who care about their neighbors.

The women accept that their anger will, to some extent, function as a constant for them. The injuries (structural and systemic injustices) toward which they orient themselves do not exist as a quick slap, then over. Abusive systems are deeply embedded in society's structure, are pervasive, and last a long time; they benefit certain people in power by their prolongation, which can make the status quo appear as "just the way things are." These injuries—the causes and stimuli of the organizers' anger—are indeed "continually multiplied." The cause of anger one day can remain a cause for anger virtually every other day.

The women not only *accept* prolonged anger, but they also actually *cultivate* it in the form of agapic anger by calling up past incidents in which they or someone they love was wrongfully injured. In a training, Mary referenced her story about her dad's measly pension and asked, "How alive do you think that story is in my gut?" Mary keeps that story alive because it mobilizes her and reminds her of what is wrong. She does not rely on only one story to do that. She has dozens of stories about why she is angry that she says need to be told "over and over so you can be motivated."

Mary chooses to experience repeated anger at past injustices. She repeatedly replays the tape. For her, the direct cause of her past anger does not need to exist anymore to be present to her awareness; she is able to access that pain of being injured through stories. Anger getting stored in accessible stories means the people do not have to carry it fulltime in their bodies.

There is a way in which the women externalize some anger. They've referred to it as a rock in their pocket, a ball, stories. It is almost like the stories carry the anger in some ways, and in revisiting the stories the anger is present again. One benefit to this practice is that when the anger is externalized in some form, then it cannot have the same access to wearing down their bodies than if it were fully or only internalized. Like writing down a schedule instead of having mentally to hold it in view all day, the women's stories hold anger that they can check out when needed.

Mary practices storytelling to replay past incidents of anger in order to access her anger. Seneca judged replaying anger-causing incidents to be morally suspect, even irrational, because of anger's many pitfalls and because he believed that no virtue could come of it.[21] Perhaps for Seneca, who seemed to have embodied considerable white, male, aristocratic privilege, virtuous enactment of anger *was* beyond his imagination. Seneca's power was routinely upheld by the prevailing social structures. Society, however, needs to hear from people who have experienced marginalization on the topic of whether prolonged access to anger is beneficial in the struggle for justice. Unlike the Stoics, the organizers do not shun anger *carte blanche*. Instead, they accept exposure to anger because they deem the good of agapic anger worth the risks. They assess the world to need the good aspects of anger too much to eliminate it from their repertoire.

Aquinas cautions against long-term anger generating hatred. Aquinas defines hatred as a long-lasting emotion that moves away from something apprehended as unsuitable or hurtful.[22] He says, "Anger is said to grow into hatred, not as though the same passion which at first was anger, afterwards becomes hatred by becoming inveterate; but by a process of causality. For anger when it lasts a long time engenders hatred."[23] The point is not that long-established and unlikely-to-change anger necessarily morphs into hatred. Rather, long-term anger *can* cause hatred if it is not well monitored.

Anger, which is an approach emotion that seeks to confront the cause of injury, experienced over a long period, can lose its approach quality, and a person can pick up, instead, a loathing of and revulsion toward the cause of injury. Should this occur, the emotion would no longer be well characterized as a form of anger, but as hatred. Long-term anger can become a harmful habit and cause a person to have a fixed repulsion to something perceived as evil.

Philosophically speaking, it is actually possible for hatred of injustice to be considered good. Aquinas says, "Now it is part of our love for our brother that we hate the fault and the lack of good in him, since desire for another's good is equivalent to hatred of his evil,"[24] and "Love and hatred are contraries if considered in respect of the same thing. But if taken in respect of contraries, they are not themselves contrary, but consequent to one another: for it amounts to the same that one love a certain thing, or that one hate its contrary. Thus love of one thing is the cause of one's hating its contrary."[25]

Justice and injustice are contrary to one another; thus, loving justice, philosophically speaking, can align with hating injustice. On Aquinas's view, structures are unjust when they are harmful to the communal good. He says that unjust structures (like a corrupt law) "are acts of violence" and should not be observed.[26] Unjust structures are harmful and need to be replaced.[27] Hatred of "a true evil, for the reason that it is incompatible with one's natural good" is not vicious.[28] While such a conclusion may feel uncomfortable, it is important to consider because it does seem that unless one stays in touch with the pain, one may lose motivation to resist chronic injustice. Hatred (as Aquinas defines it) is one emotion that can be sustained for a long time and can motivate potentially transformative actions.

Although hatred of injustice may not be blameworthy, nevertheless, the women did not speak of hating injustice. Rather, they use the term *hatred* differently than Aquinas does. It could be that, in their minds, hatred is inherently linked to callousness, ill will, and violence. Or maybe they focus on what they love, without giving what they hate the time of day.

Regardless, they speak of living as much as possible in the experience of loving justice instead of the experience of hating injustice. The women turn to anger, not hatred, to motivate and sustain practices of dismantling systemic injustice. Jenny Michaelson, who organized with Kelly, says that "Anger *moves* me. And, it's not that empathy doesn't move me; it doesn't move me as fast."

The pursuit of increased justice and resistance to ongoing injustices repeatedly expose the organizers to considerable anger. Because they are clear about many problems that surround anger, they can choose agapic anger that tends to avoid the noted pitfalls and over which they have considerable self-command. They choose to be exposed to it, to carry it, but on their own terms. They rehearse memories of anger-provoking stimuli in order to remain in touch with the real harm of injustice and maintain reliable sources of motivation in their professional lives.

They work with their anger creatively in ways that transmute pain and energy into meaningful and effective action that serves the common good. The women reason well that it is appalling to feel no pain in response to another's suffering, and they have noticed that anger energizes them for justice work. Doing this work together often brings them joy, expressed in energy, laughter, and contentment.

PART IV

Choreography of Agapic Anger

Working with anger has been described as a sort of dance. This dance often is born out of necessity. People who want something better for their communities can feel depressed when they bump up against systems that benefit dominant people or groups and therefore protect the status quo. Gaslighting can muddy the clarity a minister has about the needs her surrounding community is articulating. The challenge becomes finding ways to maintain both critical distance and investment. Through a choreography of sorts, the women organizers transform their anger into a virtuous thing that leads toward the justice their communities need and is healthy for them. As part of the relationship-building so central to community organizing, they sometimes invite others into a set of movements that enhance people's capacity to do well by their anger.

Agapic anger is still an anger, but it is a choreographed anger—shaped through a variable combination of self-directed, relationally supported changes that predictably can yield a nuanced and communally beneficial anger. Of these constitutive elements, there is no prescribed order or complete set. In the women's experience, they exercise practical wisdom rather than following a script when they teach this improvised choreography. The elements employed will differ person to person, depending on what resources are available and what is judged most likely to be helpful under given conditions. Yet, there is an overarching direction of the movement from a more chaotic, individually oriented anger to a more deliberate, constructive anger.

Through observing the women's social choreography of agapic anger, five steps that are improvisational but tend to weave together familiar elements emerge. Part IV introduces the five movements that constitute the choreography the women informally teach as well as practice. The women expect themselves to move through a process similar to that through which they lead others in order that both their own emotions and the emotions of others align well with particular chosen actions. Through nonidentical repetitions of a reflection–action cycle the organizers transform anger, and through this process the organizers are transformed.

Chapters 11 and 12 describe a reflection–action model by which the women facilitate a transformation of anger. Chapter 11 shows how early movements toward agapic anger tend to begin in a phase of reflection, which engenders reflexivity and awareness leading to self-knowledge. The reflection phase includes agitating, aiming anger well, and connecting. Chapter 12 portrays the action phase that includes both motivating action and acting itself. The chapter notes the work of neuroscientist Richard Davidson and philosophers Myisha Cherry and Judith Barad because they each examine how anger energizes or motivates people; Cherry and Barad go further to argue that anger often motivates prosocial action.

Kelly's narrative in chapter 10 helps illuminate the process of transforming anger into agapic anger. Her story also reflects the ways that she operates simultaneously as organizer, academic, and religious leader—someone who loves processes to the point that when she talks about them, people leave convinced that working the process could do more for their well-being than their top three self-care practices combined. More than anyone, Kelly teaches consistently about the process of the organizing cycle. Furthermore, Kelly intentionally brings up issues of intersectionality (overlapping forms of marginalized identities). Each person's intersectionalities, along with their immunities from marginalizations complicate how anger will function in their life.

CHAPTER TEN

Find the Gap

Meet Kelly Marciales

The speed of her gait outstrips many people's but matches the pace of her speech and wit. While Kelly Marciales is herself on the move, she also is profoundly committed to the transformative movement of the leaders she cultivates. She is just the person to emphasize transformation because it is authentic to her own life journey. It began with her elders.

Before World War II, when New Year's came around, her grandparents, who practiced Shintoism, set out plates of mochi rice and tangerines and lit incense in honor of the ancestors. Her grandfather was born in California in 1918 into a family who knew the hard labor of the peasant class of farmers in Japan. Her grandmother, born in 1923, also in the United States, had different roots—she was samurai. Her father, being the fourth son of a samurai and therefore unlikely to inherit, deemed his prospects better in the United States and emigrated. "They grew up speaking Japanese as a primary language."

As children, her grandparents were forced by the US government to move from their birthplaces near Terminal Island, California—just feet from the Pacific Ocean between Long Beach and San Pedro in the greater Los Angeles area—to Rohwer, Arkansas. An internment camp bounded by a swamp and fenced with razor wire awaited them. There they lived "from the fall of '42 to six months after [the War Relocation Authority] closed down the camp. So they voluntarily stayed—lots of Japanese voluntarily stayed in the camps and were allowed to stay in the camps after the war until they can find jobs and housing, which was difficult to find because they had been moved from the West coast all the way to Arkansas." Rohwer closed November 30, 1945.

No longer having access to their property in California, around May 1946 Kelly's grandparents moved to Chicago, where they had acquaintances with some apartment space. "If someone got an apartment first, then they'd invite a couple of families in to stay in this tiny apartment until they could find other housing."

After the war her grandparents felt pressure to deemphasize their Japanese and Shinto roots. "My family made a conscious decision to assimilate. They moved to Chicago, and in that time, they decided they were no longer going to participate in observing Japanese culture. So, at the moment they moved to Chicago, they stopped speaking Japanese. They also joined a Presbyterian church, which was very common for Japanese immigrants to do, and they stopped associating with Japanese."

Kelly aptly calls out what happened during and after World War II as loss of culture. "It was unjust. There was no reason for it, and at the same time, it happened, and it happened for years. And nobody really rose up and did anything about it." Along with many families, Kelly's wondered how they were going to prevent future internment and hate against Asian Americans. "They were grasping at 'What can we do?'—thinking that they had done something to cause that [internment], to cast doubt [on their fidelity to the United States]. So, their reaction to being in prison was, 'Somebody, somewhere must have done something. We've got to stop being too Japanese so that when they ask us, "Who do we swear allegiance to?" (even though you were born in Southern California), "Do you swear allegiance to Japan or to the United States?" You're going to say, "I don't even know how to speak Japanese. My name's . . ." (like my uncle's name is Randall Wayne) "My name is Randall Wayne. I don't speak Japanese."' So that loss of culture was their response to try and keep themselves safe for the next time. It was a collective choice that these individual families were making—their own way to organize themselves. They felt at the time that that was what they needed, that that would in some way benefit their next generation. . . . So just keep your head down."

Kelly's grandparents eventually did move back to Los Angeles, where "they joined another Presbyterian church, and they were Presbyterian all throughout my dad's childhood. I think that was for the sake of the boys," because after her dad and uncle graduated high school, her grandparents stopped attending. Only years later did her grandmother start going to a Methodist congregation with her niece, whose husband was the pastor.

Kelly did not grow up Christian; she was a vocal atheist. "I had a really dramatic conversion experience when I was seventeen. I was an atheist, and I had a group of friends that were also atheists, and we had gone to an atheist convention. At that convention I attended a workshop where we were learning to use Scripture to debunk Christian arguments. So, I was given a Bible at an atheist convention and a list of Scriptures to go home and study. And when I was reading through the Gospel of John, God spoke to me. And so, I freaked out. I threw the book—kind of sat there wondering whether or not I was having some sort of like psychotic break. And after a little while I went back and picked up the book and realized that there, indeed, had been some change in that when I was reading the book before I heard God speak, it was like reading a textbook. But then, when I went back to the book afterward, it was—all I can describe it as—like the words sang. It was full of meaning and was powerfully and prophetically speaking *to* me, not dry like a textbook way.

"But it did take me quite a while to get invited to a church. I kept asking Christian people in my school that I knew were Christian, 'Hey, can I go to church with you one day?' And they thought, because I was such an outgoing, outspoken atheist, that I was screwing with them. And so, I really had a hard time getting an invite to church, and I didn't want to just start going to churches because, honestly, there was a part of me that thought, 'What if something really bad happens when I walk into a church?'" Kelly started attending a nondenominational "rock-and-roll type" church. One Sunday her would-be husband went with her.

> He just had this face like, "Oh, this is a church?"
> "Okay, where do you want to go?"
> "I'd really like to go to a Methodist church."
> "Oh, is that like hymns and organs and stuff?"
> He said, "Yeah, I like that."
> I'm thinking, "Oh God, it's going to be awful."

So, Kelly took him to a Methodist church her grandma was attending. "It was okay. What really astounded me was that people *saw* us." The congregation didn't focus on surface things; "they asked real, personal, getting-to-know-you questions—not superficial and make-you-uncomfortable kinds of questions. They cared about our daughter; they also said, 'Oh that's your grandma!'

"My time at the Methodist church has deepened my faith, but going through the process of becoming a deaconess really is where I've grown exponentially in my faith." Kelly is now a consecrated deaconess in the Order of Deaconesses and Home Missioners in the United Methodist Church—having earned her degree while being a full-time organizer.

Their United Methodist congregation in Huntington Beach, California, worked to promote LGBTQ+ inclusion ahead of the 2012 General Conference (GC12), the annual, national, denomination-wide governing body. "The LGBT community and its allies really thought that they were going to pass some legislation that was going to have inclusive language," but the General Conference voted the proposal down. "The lament and anger that came after those who had gone to 2012 General Conference got home—that [anger] felt right. It felt *earned*. And they weren't angry *at* the bishops or angry *at* that white man or that group of people or whatever. They were sad, lamenting, but they were angry." The congregation's anger was directed at "systemic injustice. And we actually had a prayer service the first Sunday after that General Conference, and we just read from some of the songs crying out to God. And it was one of the most powerful things I've ever seen."

USING ORGANIZING AS A TOOL

Kelly's path into community organizing began, as she recalls it, with a major move for her husband's work. Kelly moved in November 2013 with the whole family from Huntington Beach, California, to Palmer, Alaska, in the Mat-Su Borough.[1] "The people are different [in California and Alaska]—and in both good and bad ways." From the taxi driver to the hotel staff to the realtor, people were kind and generous, but racism was also present in ways beyond what they'd experienced before. "[I] never experienced racism really in California because I grew up in the racial bubble of California. Everybody looked like me or was darker. So, it wasn't really a thing that I contended with. So, moving up here, all of a sudden there was language that I had never heard before. As a stay-at-home mom, there's no perceived power, and so there was no pushback. But then as I gained more power in the community, there was pushback, there was critique and there were roadblocks."

By January they had joined a church. "By July 2014 [the pastor] invited my husband and our kids over for a bonfire, and he handed me a book."

[Pastor] said, "Have you ever thought about community organizing?"

I said, "I don't even know what that is."

And he said, "Oh, well, here's the book. I want you to read it. It was *Doing Justice* by Dennis Jacobson." It's basically just the manual—110 pages of the organizing cycle.

"So, I read it. I never read anything like it before. The ideas in this book, the whole organizing model, challenged everything that I understood, both politically and theologically." By October Kelly had been invited to her first four-day AFACT (Anchorage Faith and Action Congregations Together) training. She landed AFACT's internship. While Kelly suspected she'd work for AFACT, longer-term leaders envisioned her building VIA (Valley Interfaith Action) in the Mat-Su Borough. Kelly got looped in when it was grant-writing time; she got grants, applied for VIA to become a 501c3, rewrote articles and bylaws from a parent organization, and filed with the state. Kelly was hired as VIA's first executive director and lead organizer. "It was a hard transition though because I went from having an established organization [AFACT] with established leaders—sixteen congregations. Then, all of a sudden, I had nothing. I started from scratch. Nobody knew what we were—other than the few pastors that were at the table. . . . So, some of that work was extraordinarily difficult because nobody had ever heard of community organizing, period. And if they had, they had a negative, very negative connotation. I was called a communist, a socialist."

Kelly began her time at VIA with hundreds of one-to-ones in the first year so that she could listen to this new community and adapt the model she'd learned in response to this particular place. For Kelly, one-to-ones are a place "where I see God. It is what brings me to this work. There is a holy space that's created when two people come together and are vulnerable in this way: sharing pain, lamenting, and receiv[ing] a non-manipulative gift of listening." Kelly was intentional about the one-to-ones. "I really believed in this work, and I also know that this work is dangerous to the people who have power right now. So, how do we build a relationship so that we can do this work together?"

Each congregation that is a member of VIA casts its own vision by working through a process of discovery by naming the discrepancy between the world as it is and the world as it could be. "I don't tell them; they name what they see wrong in the world." Leaders within each congregation then work the organizing cycle in relation to what the people specifically have named as going awry and the hope they hold that the situation could be different.

After five-and-a-half years as executive director of VIA, establishing the network, growing leaders, and equipping congregations to run the organizing cycle, Kelly was called by the ELCA to be the program coordinator in charge of faith-based community organizing and the director of organizing for Mission (positions held by Sue Engh before her retirement). About four years into this position, when the churchwide organization was not living the antiracism values they professed, Kelly's clarity about her own values—born, in part, out of leading the values training for organizers for years—made it plain that a change was in order. She accepted the role of director of the Kellogg Campus of Alaska Pacific University, where she implements and sustains ecologically and culturally responsive educational programs. A sought-after community organizing instructor, she can accept only a fraction of the invitations to teach that she receives, and she continues to be invigorated by preparing seminary students to grow in their use of organizing tools for ministry.

POWERFUL JESUS, POWERFUL RELATIONSHIPS

Kelly reflects on the many religions and philosophies that influenced her understandings of anger. She is clear that separating out the religious influences from other cultural influences is impossible as well as artificial. "Being raised in a family where Shinto/Buddhist and Confucianist philosophy were the undercurrent of our family values and behavior, anger was not acceptable." Being reflexive, Kelly notices that what she has access to is "Japanese American culture as I've understood it through osmosis. I wasn't explicitly taught any of this; it's just that absorbed culture you just get from living. . . . I don't know, but as far as I'm aware, there's no such thing as a good time for you to be angry and act against something in Buddhism because it's all about creating harmony, and how you create harmony is by creating peace, and you create peace either by passivity—by not engaging—which is why, when I started doing this work it was really hard for my grandparents. So, I had to package it in such a strange way; basically, I just said, 'I work for the church developing leaders.' I left out all the pieces where I'm challenging authority and how our political system operates and doing civic engagement. I left all of that out because that would be fundamentally opposed to our family values.

"Asian families [can ignore] disputes for the sake of perceived peace. Men are the only ones really allowed the right to anger, and that is still seen as bad form, but acceptable." Kelly knew from experience that her dad was allowed anger. "My dad was very expressive about his anger, even to my grandparents, definitely to me—verbally and physically abusive to me. So if my dad were to start really laying into me verbally and if I were to say anything in retort, everyone at the family dinner table would shut that down. Being a woman—being a girl child and being younger—you absolutely don't [counter]. That oppressive feeling about how you don't do anger pretty much set the tone for understanding how anger plays out in our family dynamic. So, if someone—Dad—wants to blow up at you, you just let them do that. You don't engage it. And then it'll be done, and then you just go on.

"Any time things got hard, it wasn't like, 'Fight back!' or 'Stand up for yourself!' It was *gaman*.[2] I understand it through a Japanese folk tale that I was told." There's no direct translation in English. The National Endowment for the Arts 2010 exhibit "The Art of Gaman: Arts and Crafts from the Japanese American Internment Camps, 1942–1946" said, "*Gaman* means to bear the seemingly unbearable with dignity and patience."[3] "It's this idea that things in life are hard, and that it's a virtue to *gaman*." That's how Kelly grew up understanding hardship, from which she has developed her own nuanced view. "*Gaman* is so important in my life because there are many things where I still practice that. In fact, it's more of an active engagement in choosing *when* to protest. I think my default setting before was to *gaman* always—like the Japanese with the internment—*gaman* was what Japanese people did during the internment. Now, I will *gaman* personally or interpersonally, but I do not *gaman* in a collective injustice."

Kelly's early experiences within Christianity also impacted her views on anger. "I read the Bible for the first time when I was seventeen years old. 'If there is anger in your heart, you've committed murder.' Not growing up in the church or with a Christian family, Jesus seemed to have a passive theology to me, dotted with weird episodes of passionate anger (table-flipping, mass killing of Gerasene pigs, and tree-cursing). The evangelical, nondenominational megachurch I attended focused on personal holiness and passivity, love of self, and abolition of sin—particularly in others so you could bring them to church."

Kelly's early, embedded understandings of anger made for a slow process as she shifted toward appreciating the importance of anger in public life.

She now says, "Anger is not a forbidden sin but an expression of disapproval of injustice and a tool that binds communities together against regimes, monarchies, idolatry, false nationalism, sexism, racism, and other systemic injustices that permeate our lives."

As a United Methodist deaconess who trains faith-based community organizers, Kelly points trainees toward biblical stories like the daughters of Zelophehad who, in a patriarchal system that made no provision for their inheritance, seek the land rights of their deceased father. "They stood before Moses, Eleazar the priest, the leaders, and all the congregation, . . . 'Why should the name of our father be taken away from his clan because he had no son? Give to us a possession among our father's brothers'" (Numbers 27:2a, 4). She will also lift up a story from the book of Esther. "Mordecai challenges Esther. He's frustrated with Esther's, 'Oh, I don't know if I'm going to do this.' [Mordecai's] angry because she is in a position of power and influence to be able to do something. 'So, if not you, who?' And that comes from a place of anger and frustration. That's not from an, 'Oh, sweetheart . . .' I mean, it's not from a compassionate or empathetic place, but from a place of frustration, anger.

"I do not use God and anger. Ever. 'Cause I don't think God is an angry God. That is not the God that I know. God that I know is the God who hates injustice but does not hate people groups. So, you will not hear me use anything where God is angry. I never want anyone to lose their faith in God because of the work that we do. All I want for them is to understand their faith more deeply through acting in a just way."

There are times at VIA where Kelly wants leaders to mobilize around their anger. She might ask, "'What'll happen if we do nothing?' and of course the answer is, 'Well, things will stay the same or they'll get worse.' Right?! There's really no other answer. But the challenge becomes, we're people of faith and if [only people] from the secular community do something about it, what does that say about the power of Christ? What does that say about the power of us, as people of faith, to get stuff done? Does that just mean that we're nice church folks and we can't get anything done? We can just sit in a room and put our hands together? We can put money in a plate? We'll just go knit quilts instead?

"No! We're powerful people.

"My experience of anger as an Asian American woman moved me from a place where I was only allowed to be a recipient of someone else's anger to a place where I am more comfortable with the role of organizer and invoking righteous anger, prophetically, to move people. The changes were most dramatic in my years as a community organizer, learning what to do with anger and processing through the discomfort of acknowledging my own anger toward injustice and unjust systems. These are the very same systems that relocated my Japanese American family in 1942 from Terminal Island, California, to Rohwer, Arkansas. These are the systems that kept my family, tenant farmers, from being homeowners. My family taught me, as many *Nisei* and *Sansei* taught their *Yonsei* generations,[4] 'Keep your head down. Don't make waves and don't ask questions.' I defy this each day I go to work, an anachronism in my own culture. Organizing changed all this. Organizing put me in close proximity to those who were hurting and [who] demanded that I not *help* them but *join* them on their *own* journey. I could not help but find my own empowerment on that path as I journeyed with others toward theirs."

CHAPTER ELEVEN

The Reflection Sequence

Initial Steps

A reflection–action sequence offers a structure by which people can help themselves and others sculpt their anger well. While the whole process begins with reflection, it can still be considered what the field of psychology has called an action–reflection model. The women's reflection–action process includes five moves that blend together in variable combinations to choreograph transformation partly in the form of feeling and consenting to one's anger and "funneling" it into strategic embodiments of love and justice. The initial reflection sequence includes the first three of these moves (agitating, aiming anger well, and connecting), and begins to shape anger toward its agapic form through many opportunities to bring anger into critical engagement with thought.

In the reflection phase, a shift happens: from amalgamations of diffuse, destructive, uncooperative, or individual angers, an agapic anger emerges that is well aimed, filtered, focused on real structural-level change, and connected to others. By working on their anger with a guide, leaders become ever more disposed, together, to a love of justice and communal flourishing. Inner- and inter-transformation are not merely side effects; they are partially constitutive of the work of social transformation. This is true not only because these transformations empower them to sustain love for the long work of changing seemingly intractable structures, but also because their own transformation is itself part and parcel of the transformation of society. As they build relationships, connect with others to build enough power to effect systemic change, and train their anger on the winnable issue they cut, the women also help dismantle abusive systems and build aspects of a new and different future.

STEP 1: AGITATIONAL UPLIFT

When organizers invest in a leader's formation and care to develop them, they offer agitational uplift, helping emerging leaders to see the disconnect between who they say they want to become and how they have been showing up. The women understand this to be one of the deepest acts of love that can be offered to another. Organizers sometimes lean into a person's articulation of anger, drilling down and helping them attain more clarity about the true source of their anger or the result they want from their anger. This often occurs through a strategy that organizing networks have called *agitation*. In her book, Sue presents agitation as "the most effective relational tool for moving a person from where they are to where they need to be."[1] Agitations land when they expose the gap between what a person says she values about herself or the world and how she acts. Therefore, agitation can help a person deepen her self-awareness and align with her deepest concerns and commitments. Sue identifies four steps in a typical agitation:[2]

1. Articulating the self-interest or values the person holds related to a given situation.
2. Identifying their behavior that is contradictory to their self-interest or values.
3. Helping them understand the consequences of their behavior for themselves and others around them.
4. Getting a commitment from them to adjust their behavior to fit their values and self-interest.

The first time Sue met Mary they were at a training Mary was leading. Mary "began to work the space, moving up and down the aisles, frequently leaning in close to address individual participants."[3] Sue recalls that Mary blended group training with person-specific agitations. Sue says,

> As I watched and waited, vicariously impacted by Mary's challenges to my peers, I was aware of a growing excitement in my belly, a quickening of my heart rate, a rising flush to my face. I simultaneously hoped

and feared that she would come my way and address me directly. When she eventually did, I remember setting down my pen to face her, smiling warily. She began her engagement with me by saying, "You've been awfully quiet, Reverend. What's going on for you?" As she worked me over for the next several minutes, I remember thinking that I had never before been taken so seriously by someone who didn't know me! I remember feeling, as a result of the encounter, convicted yet affirmed, challenged yet accepted, judged yet validated.[4]

Sue thinks, "By daring to agitate me and others to be transformed into the leaders God intends for us to be, those who practice it exhibit one of the most powerful forms of love that I know."[5]

The term *agitation* does not immediately convey the best parts of what the skill entails, so the phrase "agitational uplift of authenticity" may be better aligned for the following set of reasons. First agitational uplift is loving someone enough to call them into their own deepest, authentic, remarkable, and actionable selfhood. This movement is a marvelous gift, yet requires nuance to land as gift.

A second reason to adjust the name comes from postcolonial, womanist, antiracist, Queer, and feminist critique and exposes something that organizing networks in the United States didn't necessarily get when the term *agitation* and practice were created. When a person in a structural position of power—whether that be the trainer, or a white, cishet, straight, highly educated, and so on, person—incompetently agitates someone who doesn't have a thick armor of dominant privileges, harm can occur. Accumulations of previous sidelining, violation, diminishment, and so much more exist between the two people long before they are face to face. US culture has trained people with dominant positionalities to be unaware of many complex realities and life experiences that exist for people inhabiting multiple intersectionalities.

Third, trainings with seminarians have been revealing that the previous agitation technique, when done among relative strangers and with anything less than practiced excellence are repeatedly not going well. There is not adequate research to say why this is. Research might find that one contributing factor may be something that is a growing strength in US culture. Incoming seminarians are increasingly capable of sensing how they're feeling, honoring what they notice, and identifying power differentials as potentially problematic. Increased mutuality is a growing expectation.

Fourth, the implicit denotation people feel when they hear the word *agitation* is negative, but what women want to do with this skill is positive and life-affirming. The word *agitation* does a good job of getting at the fact that this skill can leave a person feeling disrupted inside because it makes a person question if they want to keep behaving in a certain way. The word *agitation*, as it is heard in current US culture, misses the main point of this skill and instead sounds like an unpleasant state of anxiety. That misses the mark because this skill is used to try to fully see people, to love the deep capacity and goodness a trainer sees in them, to hold up a mirror that shows their behaviors, and to invite them to step into their own liberation.

The word *uplift* denotes more clearly the main point of this skill, which is a profound gift of being taken seriously, believed in, and called to act authentically. Agitational uplift of *authenticity* calls a person into deeper genuineness. Being called into increased congruence can feel disruptive because it suggests a person was holding back on their full authenticity. The phrase *agitational uplift* will be used here; at the same time, the organizers' direct quotes remain unchanged, since *agitation* is the current term in the field.

Sue provides a general example of what agitational uplift might look like. "An organizer might say, 'You know, everything you say to me tells me you want such and such to happen or you want to be so and so in the world, but yesterday when we were at the meeting you behaved like this, and that was really different from what you say you want for yourself. Is that how you want to come across?' And usually people will get fairly defensive and say, 'That's not what I meant . . .' But you hold up a mirror and say, 'That's what happened. . . . I think you are capable of so much more. Do you want to become different? How can I help?'"

Sue was quick to point out that "to be a purist about agitation," one would have to acknowledge that agitation itself includes both a critical move and an affirming move. In an agitation "you make a judgment about what's not working for me, and you are supposed to have a counter judgment about how clear it is to you that I can live up to a greater standard. There's supposed to be two judgments: 'Here is what I know you're capable of, 'cause either I've seen it, or I just know it's what you want. But here's what's happening, and it's not a good match.'"

Not surprisingly, people can feel vulnerable when receiving public, agitational uplift. While organizers are not striving to make people defensive, they recognize that defensiveness is a common response, and they affirm its value if it opens to greater self-awareness. They have experienced this practice as liberation and a catalyst to think and act differently. Mary was changed the first time she was agitated, in this case by a male trainer. As she tells it, she initially rejected what he'd seen. "This guy doesn't know what he's talking about." But a couple of hours later she knew he had named what she had avoided seeing for herself. She reflects, "It was probably the most pivotal experience in my life. It led me—it didn't do it immediately—but it ultimately led me into leadership and becoming an organizer. You know, the greatest gift anyone could ever give you is to agitate you."

Agitational uplift has the power to wake people up to the difference between who they say they are and how they are acting, between what they say they care about and how they invest their life. Organizers endeavor for their agitational uplifts to be truly open so that people can freely agree or disagree with their assessments.[6] Agitational uplift invites people to commit themselves to living more fully into who they say they want to be. Uplift around anger often presses people to ask what good their anger does, to challenge people around ineffective or self-consuming anger, to clarify the goal of their anger and assess whether that is consistent with the people they want to be.

Drea offers an example that shows how an agitational uplift is rooted in people's values and what is best for them given their ties to their communities. "So you know we have a whole training on agitation: you do your relational meeting with them. You find out what self-interest they have. You share your own self-interest. And as you're developing that relationship, you understand what they care about and what makes them angry. Like, for example, I'm working with a single mom who can't get any tutoring for her son. So, when I hear that they're going to close more tutoring on the south side, then I'm gonna go talk to that parent if they say there's a public comment period where you can hand in your opinions. I would go to the parent and say, 'Hey, Sally, you remember when you're talking about how you had a hard time getting tutoring for Darren? And you have to travel three buses and one train just to get tutoring for him? Well, imagine if that one goes away and you have to go even further.' 'Oh, no!' They start getting angry right? Then I say, 'Okay, well, what are we going to do about it?' (So the anger comes from their self-interest. They care about something. It's a value. If they don't care about it, and they're not willing to act on it, it's not a value.) You say something like, 'Do you care about it enough to act on it?' (And that's what we consider values.) So you tap into their values, and you may have to use agitation. We talk about agitation in different ways. There's irritation, right? You can irritate people. We're not irritating people. We're not trying to make them angry. We agitate them to the point where they want to do something about it."

Agitational uplift can, but does not need to, involve anger. What defines it is this: in seeing a person's excellence and caring for her well-being as a person in community, you hold up what she says she values alongside a chance to act congruently.

Some people can learn how to critically uplift themselves so that they notice gaps between what they say they want/who they say they are and how they are behaving. This is very different from a negative inner critic. It is imperative that self-agitation, just like agitational uplift for leaders, is done with a healthy love of self and belief in self.

STEP 2: AIM ANGER WELL

Anger needs to get aimed where it belongs by filtering out self-shaming, other-blaming and additional unconstructive angers, focusing disorganized or dissipating angers, moving toward a particular realistic change, and recalibrating anger from forms that are preoccupied with an individual toward forms directed at structures that are responsible for chronic human suffering. While anger already is present for many people due to life experiences and injustices in the world, that anger is often buried, poorly or unintentionally aimed, and, therefore, somewhat chaotic. Anger can be felt well only when it takes up an appropriate target.[7] Agapic anger, as the women enact it, tends away from abusive systems and toward social transformation. This section shows three tactics (filtering and focusing, choosing realistic change, and recalibrating) by which the women invite people to train their anger against a particular injustice in their community and toward the social transformation that could alleviate the suffering specific to that injustice.

Filter and Focus

Part of transforming initial and assorted angers into agapic anger includes filtering out unwanted angers and focusing remaining angers. Unfitting angers can be filtered so that people refuse certain angers unbecoming of the person's character, shift or rein in other angers to align with better goals, and build on still other angers that are well focused on abusive systems and needed transformation. Although filtering anger can result in its dismissal, it often leads to redirection. Different amounts or sorts of work are needed depending on whether angers present are vicious, vague, or advisable.

Drea Hall indicates that aiming for revenge is a red flag. On the south side of Chicago, Drea works with a lot of young people whose backs are forced up against a wall by systemic poverty and racism. After telling a story about some youth turning to weapons for revenge, she says, "We need to figure out a way to funnel their anger into activism, like art activism. We had an event a couple of weeks ago and there were some young ladies there—Reverend Jen brought two of the young girls from the dance group, and they were children of immigrants, and they were angry. They talked, they gave testimony, and, then, they danced. Man, and I was like, 'Was I that angry when I was young?' But if I'd seen my father get dragged out and never had seen him again, I'd be pretty angry, too. They're like, 'We express ourselves through art and dance.' I love that concept of using their anger: they recognize their anger; they have a right to be angry; then how do we use that anger to change the world?"

Drea sees that the youth have good reason to be angry because they are growing up oppressed by racism, poverty, immigration injustice, and so on. She affirms directing their anger into strategic action aimed at exposing harmful systems. The youth who danced despite or because of being separated from their immigrant parents assert a claim that they will not be undone by the US "justice" system—a claim that "through art and dance" they will be seen, that they will be here, that they will build on their gifts. These dancing paragons of strength might be making many apt claims: the immigration system in the United States is broken, serves to increase their invisibility, and carries blame for contributing to the precarity of their lives. Yet their aim is not vengeance; what they want is to be seen, to grow up healthy with possibilities, and to have adults reconsider why they themselves are not acting for immigration reform. They deserve to be recognized for their excellence and powerful potential. Drea sees the dancers aiming their anger well.

On Drea's view, the youth's resistance dance had the capacity to "change the world," which suggests that their anger was focused well and had enough power to right some wrong (which is not yet equivalent to righting all the wrongs they had endured).[8] Audre Lorde writes, "Focused with precision [anger] can become a powerful source of energy serving progress and change."[9] Drea, who recognizes the very real option of weaponizing anger, sees that focusing anger through dance on social commentary about immigration reform does change the world whether others appreciate that fact or not. The dancers' resistance to reduction, investment in community, prosocial outlet, and artistic beauty improve the world.

Drea, in her story about the teens' resistance dance, suggested that violent anger that turns to weapons is not the sort of anger to which she would consent. At the same time, Drea did not seem to think that anger needed to be discarded, but, rather, it could be redirected. She said, "We need to figure out a way to funnel their anger." The daughters of deported immigrants are funneling their anger well. They have a right to recognize their anger as anger (not having to clothe it as sadness or fear), to express their anger, and to have unjust systems challenged in the face of their anger.

Given the positive difference Drea expects anger can make, she wants to redirect her own into organizing and community-based support. She has seen redirection work for others; she has also lived it. Already angry at the structures of racism and poverty that so constrained her life prospects, she says, "I got into organizing and it was okay to be angry. It was okay to recognize that you're angry, which to me meant that you cared. And then what do we do about it? And what I love about organizing is that I have a place to funnel some of my energy—good or bad—and I can funnel it to do good things that hopefully impact thousands." Drea notices that regardless of how well or poorly aimed the initial surge of her anger was, it came with energy, which could be directed to the good—to social transformation in the direction of affordable housing and changing legislation around the criminal legal system.

Kathy Bishop, a leader with VIA, finds that she needs to shift destructive forms of anger into something positive. "Maybe it is my age [seventy-two], but destructive anger takes too much energy. It isn't worth the energy it takes to hold onto. When I can turn anger into a positive like organizing, where I am helping others have a voice, it becomes exciting and energizing." She finds it freeing that once she has focused some anger into organizing, she no longer has to feel that prior acidic anger. Choreographing anger into its prosocial form offers an outlet for would-be destructive anger.

Kelly and Sue recognize their role in also helping future leaders to focus their existing anger. Kelly says, "Our people are pissed, but they're pissed right now unharnessed." Sue reflects that people can learn "how to channel [anger] in a way that can be helpful." Organizers endeavor to help people gain clarity about where to expend energy. Filtering anger helps people walk away from detrimental forms of anger and build on prosocial ones. By focusing anger, organizers help people direct initial surges of anger to the good, embrace healthy outlets for anger, and become clear regarding advantageous places to expend anger.

Choose Realistic Change

Unfocused anger needs to be directed and can be well aimed. In general, agapic anger tends away from abusive systems and toward social transformation. The women are yet more specific in their aims. They insist that what they spend their (and others') energy moving toward needs to be, in their words, winnable.[10] People do better by their anger when the anger is trained in such a way that it moves toward realistic change because choosing too large or amorphous a problem can lead too easily to disappointment and can stymie proactive movement. The women help people pinpoint a specific, realistic change within a particular unjust structure or select some concrete enhancement of communal flourishing that they want.

Moving toward realistic change honors people by caring that they use wisely the energy it takes to experience and express anger well. As the women see it, anger is at their disposal, but it takes energy to wield it, so they direct it at significant matters. Mary has anger at the ready. "I feel like I carry it in my pocket and pull it out whenever the hell I need it." Yet, she consciously decides if and when to pull out her anger.

Mary recounts being at a meeting of a national organization where she "raised the whole issue of diversity because that's why they brought me on. They wanted me to help them diversify their board and diversify their organization. And nominations came up for the executive committee and I raised it up that I certainly hoped that this executive committee was going to reflect some diversity in age, in race or ethnicity, in gay or lesbian people. . . . So, out comes the announcement and they're all white and they're all over sixty-five years old. So, I go to the next board meeting, and they announced it just as a report, and I raised my hand. I raised it and I said, 'This is a disgusting and embarrassing report. And I just want to say that if you're a board member who sat here a year and a half ago and voted up the diversity plan, then you must vote down this nomination.'"

It is a longer story, but in the next weeks it was at times uncertain whether the nominating committee would come back with a more diverse palette of candidates. In addition, the chair reprimanded Mary, saying that she had exhibited anger and offended some board members. She thought, "I don't give a crap . . . because I'm gonna choose where I put my energy to fight and your organization's not going to be the place I'm gonna do it in. 'So, you decide; if you're going to use me to help diversify, fine . . .' And I'm thinking, am I going to pull my anger out of my pocket for this one? Absolutely not. I'm not going to do it because I'm not in this for the long haul. So, I told the chairperson, I said, 'I know I can go to your annual meeting, and I can create havoc. I know I can, and I have the right to do it.' I said, 'But what's the payoff? Just a lot of angry, middle-class, conservative white people? Not worth it. You know, you guys decide whatever you want, and I will decide whether I stay on the board or not.' So, these are times you come up with a situation and you say, 'Am I gonna invest my anger here?' My anger only has so much energy—I'm seventy-seven, right?! And so, I say, 'Do I want to invest it here? Hell no. Not here.' And so, there's a lot of places where I don't invest it and a whole lot of other places where I'm ready."

Mary is neither going to direct her anger toward issues that are not winnable nor toward winnable issues that are not worth the expenditure of her energy, bounded as it is by human limitations. Mary looked at the women around our table and laid out her conclusion. "Organizers, you've got to have it available to you when you need it"—have anger on hand; but be discerning about when it gets used. "Why would I invest it in a place where there's no payoff? Why do it?"

Mary's decision of whether to expend the energy that doing anger well takes seems based on how invested she is and if the "payoff" warrants the energy it will take. (Remember that payoff contrasts payback. Whereas payback-anger seeks retribution aimed at the perceived abuser, payoff seeks some benefit aimed at liberation from abusive systems or social transformation.) With respect to investment, Mary sometimes asks herself, "Is it my fight?" She had gotten involved with this organization at the state level because she had worked with them on disability issues, which matter greatly to her because of her brother Bobby, but the national level of the organization had neither the deep relationships based on doing projects together nor the focus on practical work on behalf of those with disabilities. Her work with the national level was less directly rooted in her fight for the people and things she loves. Mary consciously and deliberately invests anger where she deems it is going to "pay off."

Payoff does not have to benefit only others; individuals' own best interest is also valuable and attended to as they, for example, gain satisfaction in being effective and grow as people. For example, consider the teen dancers aiming anger at immigration injustice. They simultaneously can name problems with the immigration system, refuse weapons as an easy go-to, and resist sliding into despair, depression, or dread. The dancers' anger focused through dance pays off if it helps them find new friendships, be resilient today, or impacts legislation—their anger is full of value regardless of who gets to assess "success" in "changing the world."

Recalibrate to the Political Level

"You have to politicize [your anger]!" Mary declares. From her perspective, people need to level up their anger so it becomes political, where "political" means that which concerns the *polis*—the city, the community ("political" is not about partisanship here). Politicizing anger adjusts focus toward social structures or patterns instead of individuals, thereby getting people in position to make lasting, systemic change. Drea reflects, "I want to impact a greater scale." Anger that takes as its goal, for example, blaming an individual does not get at the broader scale of prosocial change that Drea names.

Activist Valerie Kaur says, "I realized that anytime we fought bad actors, we didn't change very much. But when we chose to wield our swords and shields to battle bad systems, that's when we saw change."[11] Some forms of anger focused internally or interpersonally can tear a person apart. The organizers dissuade people from angers that align with sinking into a mire. Adjusting anger away from the individual level protects people from anger consuming them; aiming anger systemically tends to be more productive.

The women advise leaders against targeting another individual with anger when it is actually a system that created the problem. Anger spent on one person when a system perpetuates the offense is of limited benefit because, even should that one person change, little difference has been gained in terms of systemic change. Sue reasons, "You know, I could be angry at these particular men in my life who have perpetuated patriarchy, but what if they're just part of a system?" From an organizing perspective, anger usually needs to be recalibrated from a personal or interpersonal level to an institutional or structural level. Once anger is recalibrated to a political level, one's time and energy can be better spent. As Mary suggests, one can "figure out how to force the political structures."

Selecting against individual recipients of anger in favor of unjust social structures (and the collectives of people who uphold them) better ensures that the purpose of anger will be good.[12] Anger toward social structures is less likely to be distorted by personal animosity. It is more likely to reflect the critical conversations of a thoughtful group. As Aquinas puts it, human actions "have a measure of goodness from the end on which they depend."[13] In other words, part of what can be good about anger depends on its goal. Making the aim greater justice gives anger a goal that is a fundamental social good. Politicizing interpersonal anger allows someone to avoid the trap of spending all her energy seeking revenge for an individual slight while larger culpable systems remain unscathed.

Earlier Pamela said, "It's not hard to politicize it." In other words, she can move readily from her existential understanding of abandonment to seeing abandonment operative at communal levels throughout society. It is not that anger was from the start politically focused but that anger that is intensely personal can be recalibrated so that the good it seeks is likely to benefit whole populations. Mary recounts stories that offer a clearer picture of how she might, in practice, encourage people to politicize their anger. She might start, "Well, [what went wrong] isn't your fault. And a lot of times we refuse to acknowledge whose fault it is. For example, people who were abused as children: I say to them. 'Where were your parents? Or teachers? You know! Where were your grandparents? Where were the neighbors? Why didn't they defend you? Where was the system? The public school system? Where were they, that this could happen to you . . . so openly, right? And no one stepped in.'

"And why aren't you angry at *them*? Instead, you're angry at yourself and what happened to you? And you're asking yourself, 'What did *I* do to deserve that?' And at the age of three, what might you have done that would've been so terrible that you would have deserved that? Nothing! So, you're never gonna get the answer you want. So why aren't you mad at the fact that there were a lot of people around you and nobody knew."

Getting anger properly aimed "makes it political! It makes it social! It makes it communal!" Mary continues, "so to politicize [means] to get a little distance for rebuilding and then to figure out where does [the anger] really, really belong? Not on my shoulders and on my lap!"

Sue sheds light in her book on how organizers train around what they call "politicizing your anger."

> Trainers encourage you to explore how your own life has been touched, or sometimes even dictated, by misfortune or injustice. . . . As people begin to name these factors, organizers help leaders shift the narrative away from self-pity and helplessness. Together we begin to understand that most of our pain and oppression is not a result of our own poor choices but is instead tied to larger systems and cultural narratives. And, we begin to see that we are not as alone as we thought we were in our struggles, as others' stories ring familiar and true, fostering a sense of community and collective power.[14]

In order to politicize anger, people have to take a courageous and vulnerable look at their pain and at the oppressor, with a critical eye to the systems that make such pain possible, the structures that legitimize such an oppressor, and the social arrangements that benefit when personal shame or interpersonal blame take the fall instead of the system that actually bears most of the culpability. When a person or a relationship aim anger internally or interpersonally, the system that structurally perpetuates the injustice is safe to continue unabated. Unjust systems persist when people diffuse their anger in small interpersonal bursts instead of politicizing the anger toward its deeper, systemic cause. Even though anger may have started out interpersonally, the women offer people opportunities to take it public.

STEP 3: CONNECT TO BUILD POWER

Agapic anger moves leaders to join with other people who share similar goals. They connect with people both to sustain their buoyancy in these arduous journeys and to increase efficacy. A person does not force political structures on her own; she works with communities to leverage change. Because agapic anger usually deals with structures, it encounters systems that often have self-conserving inertia resistant to that which would shift power dynamics. Changes demanded by a single, isolated voice tend to be more easily ignored and less effective than those called for by groups of organized people.

Organizers help people team up to build power, where power is understood as the ability to act—to effect change. Martin Luther King Jr. says, "It is not enough for people to be angry—the supreme task is to organize and unite people so that their anger becomes a transforming force."[15] The women help people to understand that because the target that needs to be addressed is a system, groups of people coalescing to work together are most effective in changing it.

Organizers assert that power is accessed and used most effectively by organized people and organized money (or resources in general). People gather into teams through a relational process. They start with one-to-ones in order to build authentic relationships grounded in intentional listening. Sue describes some outcomes of one-to-one conversations:

> It's a concentrated period of time designed to get people talking to one another one-on-one about their lives and about what matters most to them. . . . The listening process brings to the surface interests and concerns that people have about their own lives, their congregations, and the broader community. By raising these issues and realizing that others share some of those same interests and concerns, people are more readily motivated to join together and do something about them.[16]

The women do not direct people to work on a certain issue; rather, in sharing and listening, people notice patterns of concerns that unite them. They then determine together the greatest needs that stir their collective passion. Sue's work focused on congregation-based community organizing. When determining collective passion, "house meetings" are often a next step in which the shared interests that have surfaced in one-to-ones coalesce into "particular issues and ideas that people have which a congregation might want to address."[17] Leaders may draw together their own teams of people to work on a certain task, with the leader being the link between the organizer and the team. Aligned with others who share their passion, organized groups of people build collective power for change.

Ministries need relational bonds to live as Christians in the world and participate in the mission of God. People are buoyed up through bonds with fellow leaders and team members—people who encourage the emergence of a shared love of God and justice around a specific, shared topic. "Participation in collective actions is a social process that creates organizational bonds and affective ties with fellow members and participants, which facilitate the creation of shared solidarities and identities."[18] Mary tells a story of a woman trying to organize her neighborhood to block a permit for an asphalt company because many neighbors believed the high prevalence of cancer in their area was linked to toxins from this company. While this story speaks to many of the fluid elements in the transforming anger process, it unambiguously illumines the importance of connecting with others to build power.

> Mary's cellphone rang. From the other end came, "I am so pissed. I called the mayor's office. And they called me back. And I told this woman, 'Blah, blah, blah.'" And she's going on and on for like five minutes. And this is a woman she has to meet with who's on the staff for the city council's environmental committee.
>
> And so, I listened to her and finally I said, "Can I ask you a question?" I said, "Why did you give her all your anger on that phone? Why were you not in control? Now she knows exactly how you feel, and now she thinks you're a troublemaker, and now she's going to prepare for a very defensive meeting with you. Is that in your interest?"
>
> And she said, "Oh my, you're absolutely right. I told her everything. I was really mad."
>
> I said, "I get it. But how does that help you? To use your anger so quickly, without thought, without strategy—just blurt it out? No wonder, of your neighborhood people, you don't have two hundred people. You've got like twenty."
>
> And she said, "Oh, Mary, what am I going to do? I told her so many things!"
>
> I told her what to do. "You can't walk in with an all-or-nothing attitude. You say, 'We're very concerned about this. Would you be willing to come to a meeting to talk about this?' We also want to see if there are any diseases that you're concerned about that exist in your family— how long you've lived here. Slowly they're going to start winding up. Then from the health department you get the real statistics. You compare them to other neighborhoods that don't have asphalt companies, and you say, 'Look at the difference. I mean does this make you a little bit angry?' Inside, you are steaming! But you've got to bring them up to where you are, or they won't follow you. And then once you go in there, what you do is decide, what do I want out of this meeting? What are the two things—absolutes—I have to have that they can easily give us?"

Mary affirmed this woman's anger and pointed out how her approach to anger (yelling on the phone at a person who had called to set up a meeting) decreased the power of her position by undermining her credibility and giving away her talking points, which generated defensiveness. Mary encouraged her to be more strategic so she could build power rather than abdicate it. She specifically discouraged using anger for behaviors like yelling, which alienates others from the core aim (blocking a permit and recovering a healthy environment for the neighborhood). Instead, Mary urged her to use her anger in ways that build coalitions—two hundred people instead of twenty—and help people come along with her leadership toward needed change through practices like showing empathy, inviting conversation, drawing out their concerns, displaying facts, encouraging others to care. Mary mentored her to become more disciplined with her use of anger, thereby encouraging her to acquire good habits of anger and better inclinations for related actions. Mary's coaching facilitated this woman's own emergent capacities and cooperative habits. To get to the effective change leaders desire, they draw people together through team building and fostering relational bonds.

Kelly tells a story that illustrates the emphasis that she, too, puts on collaboration for the sake of building power to increase effectiveness. Kelly and her team were working to address systems that contribute to opioid abuse in the Mat-Su. The story is split into two parts in order to let the first half reveal something about building power and the second half speak to the next step: motivating action. Kelly told it all as one flowing story, which again reveals that, as the women help people work with their anger, the elements are not discrete or rigidly linear steps but are part and parcel of the larger work of organizing they do.

> Today the place where anger is brewing—where I want to mobilize around anger—is this: I have a young man who's been reaching out to the director of OSMAP (Opioid Substance Misuse and Abuse Prevention). It's a Department of Health and Social Services—a state-level—position. He has been reaching out to this person who's going to be the target of our next action, [and he] will not call our people back. Our people are pissed, but they're pissed right now unharnessed. If there was no organizer present, they would leave this feeling like our government does not pay attention to the little people. Or "all that work for nothing!" Where I see a potential is, as an organizer my job is to observe that situation, see how

people are responding. If they're not angry . . . I have one person on that team who is like, "They're just really busy." They want to "mom" the target. "Oh, you know, they're just busy; we should back off; we should give them some space. Eventually they'll reach out to us in their time . . ." [I am] using my relationship and my understanding within that system, and organizing tools, to get them to view this circumstance differently. They have the right and the power to ask—to hold public officials accountable. And they are no different than anyone else in the community who can get audience with them. But we need to change our tactics and we need to build more power.

Part of the organizers' work is helping people reimagine what they deserve and the capacity they have to drive change. In Kelly's example, she wants her leaders to expect that they deserve a response from governmental officials. She also wants people to recognize they have the power to ask for what they need and the ability to proactively build more power as needed to appropriately be taken seriously.

In summary, as organizers agitate, help people aim their anger well, and encourage people to connect in order to build the power they need to bring about change, anger is increasingly blended with thought. In the cycle of choreographing anger, these three moves (agitational uplift, aiming, and connecting) constitute a highly reflective phase.

CHAPTER TWELVE

The Action Sequence

Concluding Steps

In organizing, it is only after a long reflective process that the transformation of anger approaches the second phase in an anger choreography reflection-action sequence. So, anger that reaches the second phase—anger deemed worth informing action—is the highly reflective type. This second phase is the action sequences with its two movements: motivating and acting. These two moves constitute the part of the cycle that performs the planned-for action. In this phase, leaders find the motivation to approach and overcome obstacles. Finally, the step arrives of letting anger have a role in fueling deliberate action against unjust systems and for social transformation.

STEP 4: MOTIVATE

Agapic anger motivates both organizers and trainees to engage in activities aimed at transformation. Since there are so many reasons not to act—people are tired or don't have much time, strong forces seek to maintain the status quo, and so on—people need motivation to act. Drea reflects on her own path into organizing and ways anger was involved: "I definitely was angry. I think they tap into your anger, and they use it to motivate you. Organizing is . . . finding people's self-interest and calling them on the carpet for it." The women do not manufacture anger; anger is already present for most people. They help people clarify what their anger is really about and hone it into a righteous thing.

After telling the story about her father, Mary immediately commented on the importance of leaders telling their own stories of struggle. "How alive do you think that story is in my gut? . . . It happened yesterday! It happened yesterday at 4:00 in the afternoon! That's how alive it is. And I keep it alive. Why do you think I keep it alive? . . . It mobilizes me every single day. Now, how many stories like that do you think I have? Dozens! I develop them on purpose because I've got to be reminded that there's shit in this world." These stories need to be told "over and over so you can be motivated." Mary does not use her anger about her dad's death and the company's deceit as a motivation to pay (someone at) the company back. She uses it to remind her of what injustices feel like and to motivate her to take action that benefits oppressed people.

Kelly's story about addressing systems that exacerbate opioid abuse in the Mat-Su shows multiple elements—filtering anger toward a specific issue, building power, but also motivating action. She continues: "What my plan is right now is I want to have a conversation with them where I say—and I've done this before—I will say in an organizing meeting with my leaders that I am angry. 'You know what? He has called this guy four times. [Another leader] has called and left messages and emailed six times over the last two months. I'm pissed. Who else? Who else is angry? Because I/we are all volunteers; this guy is getting paid a lot of money—to not answer our phone calls? I don't think so.'

"And that tends to shift people's mind a little bit because they've not yet heard—most people have not yet heard—someone speak that way about how we talk about our public officials. We could be like 'I can't believe the governor put forward this budget. Wah wah wah wah wah.' Right? But that's complaining about something but having no teeth to actually do something. But in this case, we've actually built relationships. We've done research. We have something valid, and we know how to do something about it." People recognizing their anger can provide motivation to themselves and encourage others to shift their concerns so that doing something becomes a higher priority than doing nothing and doing something effective eclipses doing something less useful.

Neuroscientists agree with what the organizers have noted. Anger activates the brain's left frontal cortex. A team of scientists led by Neus Herrero report that "based on findings of increased left brain activity [anger] produces motivation of closeness, or approach. . . . The findings support the notion that nature intends us to respond to anger in ways that increase motivation to approach what is sending heart rate up and cortisol down and left brains into thinking up creative ways to make it go away."[1] Anger is classified as an approach emotion in that, instead of stimulating retreat from an obstacle—as fear or sadness tend to do—it turns a person to face and stand up to an obstacle. Director of the University of Wisconsin's influential Laboratory for Affective Neuroscience Richard Davidson has done research on the neurological response to anger. He shows that anger can be "intrinsically rewarding, with a positive quality that mobilizes resources, increases vigilance, and facilitates the removal of obstacles."[2] Myisha Cherry relies on such research when she argues that anger leads people to do something. Anger "makes one believe that they can influence the situation and provides a desire to change the situation; when people experience anger and the brain's frontal lobe is activated and activates motivational sensors, it literally fuels us to pursue justice."[3] The women report that anger energizes and motivates them and others, and their observation aligns with neurochemical processes of anger that are centered in the left frontal cortex, priming people to act.

Sue, Kelly, and Drea share the following insights about motivating people toward action. After identifying anger as a logical reaction to a value violated, Sue says, "So, because we don't want our values to be violated, if anger is sparked in us, we are more likely to do something about the value that has been violated. [Anger] is motivating." Kelly agrees and puts it succinctly: "Anger is a motivation . . . for getting something done." Drea recognizes that anger has motivated her to actions that organize for change, and she nudges people to recognize their anger to likewise motivate them to action. "So, for me [anger is] a tool that I use to hopefully motivate them to *do* something. And I will say, 'I was angry to the point where I decided I was going to be a Department of Children and Family Services social worker.' And then I realized the system's crappy. You know, it's a never-ending cycle of social services. So, I'm like, 'No way. I'm gonna do advocacy and organizing. That's where the power's at. That's where the change happens.' So that's how I show my anger. Like my anger brought me to where I am. So, I try to hopefully prod them a little with that." When seeking to motivate others, both Kelly and Drea avoid instructing others to be angry, but, instead, they let people get in touch with their own, already present anger. They articulate their own anger at the system and invite people to check their own reactions to see if they resonate with an interior movement of anger. Organizers, perhaps primarily because of their formation around the key practice of agitational uplift, attempt to deliver truly open-ended questions where leaders are free to agree that something is true for them or disagree and dig into what is truer for them.

Professor of philosophy and ethics Judith Barad affirms anger that can bring to completion a good act. "Anger is a strong motivator, stirring up activity and arousing us to energetic action."[4] Barad argues that "consequent anger"—that is, anger following a judgment—can increase the goodness of an action by helping the person to deliver on the act they know would be beneficial. Without motivation, action is not realized. Myisha Cherry says anger often results in prosocial action: "Not only does [anger] alert me to my own self-respect, but it motivates me—given the structures, the systematic, institutional racism, sexism, whatever-ism's that exist—the anger kind of gives you this motivation to go against the powers that be. And, as a result, we have Black Lives Matter . . ."[5] The women mentor willing people to recognize disturbing energy in themselves and give it structure so that it moves them to deliberate social action.

STEP 5: ACT

Although actions like protests, sit-ins, or marches may characterize many people's impressions of community organizing, actions are actually the tip of the iceberg of what organizers do and come only after a long process of formation, mindfulness, and research. Sue describes the purpose of an action, saying, "Each action is intended to call greater public attention to the issue, to build support and influence, and to get us closer to the decision-makers we've identified, applying whatever pressure is needed to get them to make the right decision."[6] An action is a strategic movement with a high likelihood of bringing about greater communal good.

Mary speaks to the distinctive role of actions, which get people interacting with larger publics. "An action is taking people outside of their realm, into the public world to do a face-to-face with a political operative, with a congressional leader, with whomever." The action could be many more things in addition to or other than addressing an elected official. Sue gives more examples of potential actions. It might be "people testifying or demonstrating at a council or board meeting or attending a public hearing. Or the action might be in the form of mobilizing leaders to show up with a clever message to decision-makers. . . . Often the most effective and ultimate action comes in the form of a public meeting that the organization hosts, at which all the various parties related to the issue come together."[7] Kelly, Mary, Drea, and Sue help people organize particular actions, aiming to alleviate suffering, improve shared flourishing, and reveal how effective grassroots efforts can be.

Certain actions would be well characterized as expressions of agapic anger. Perhaps surprisingly, when agapic anger results in outward action, that action tends not to appear stereotypically angry; it looks well aimed, focused, invested, calibrated to the systems level, interconnected, and motivated. The elements that mark agapic anger as a distinctive form of anger give way to diverse actions. For example, Kelly's team opposed the Alaska Senate's decision to close Pioneer Home, one of three state-run homes for elderly people in Alaska. They built intentional relationships, researched, and held a series of strategic meetings. Then they targeted a particular senator with whom they had a solid relationship, along with the whole Senate Finance Committee, and won increased yearly funding plus a one-time $525,000 for Pioneer Home. They had cut a significant winnable issue and achieved their goal.

Mary names a host of actions that the anger to which she assents can make happen:

- to ground in one's values;
- to protect;[8]
- to assist in defining identity;[9]
- to license others to get comfortable understanding the source of their own anger;
- to advance important stances.

"I think [anger's] a fabulous tool that can be used for a lot of different things."

For Mary, all of these actions and the additional actions that they motivate can be expressions of agapic anger: defining a person in terms of her grit, licensing self-understanding, and grounding a person in her values. How is agapic anger expressed in outward action? Agapic anger can specifically inform communal actions when, as Mary indicates, it defines, licenses, protects, grounds, and advances a person or group.

People who work regularly with anger are not surprised that anger can result in constructive civil action. Soraya Chemaly writes, "People who are able to process their anger and make meaning from it are more creative, more optimistic. They have more intimacy. They're better problem-solvers. They have greater political efficacy."[10] People who find healthful ways to express anger behave in many ways that are helpful to society. With so much prosocial capacity possible, it is a remarkable asset to have another adult, like a church leader or organizer, take people's anger seriously, helping them to develop it in light of deeply held values. The sundry behaviors motivated by agapic anger tend to look like the responsible behaviors of a healthy, confident, engaged person.

Conclusion

People who seek social transformation for the good of their communities need some agapic anger. Since society is not currently cut out to teach the people how to anger well—especially people who most need systems to stop reinforcing marginalizations and start working better for them—it is left to change-makers and justice-seekers to coach one another in the art of choreographing aimless angers into a justice-inflected love. The stories and processes in this book provide a powerful way of moving personal anger to a structural level where it can be both diffused from one's internal life and effective in creating systemic change.

God's beloved people and creation suffer—an affront to Jesus and a provocation to Christians. In a world with structural brokenness, agapic anger is necessary for the good Christian life. This anger that is vital to Christian vocation convicts Christian leaders to listen, learn, and join with others in God's work of liberation and healing for this world. This agapic anger supports the teaching and formation ministries of faith leaders and organizers and is of exceeding value in living faith beyond niceness by becoming accomplices in God's orientation toward justice. In fact, not having access to anger is a sort of social tranquilizer, incapacitating people from following a revolutionary Jesus who has a preferential option for the poor. Agapic anger is not a destroyer. What can destroy is being prohibited from anger's clarity and energy that help one name oppression and point to God's ways of freedom. Anger is not morally wrong; it is an honest, valid, embodied response to the distance between some harmful realities in our world and God's kindom.

Life is going to present unjust obstacles that constrain personal and communal flourishing—obstacles in front of which it would be reasonable to quail, to quit. Women have been and continue to be at risk of losing status, income, friends, and more if they eschew social norms by enacting anger in ways that are deemed unbecoming of them. This dynamic is amplified by the fact that women come up short on position and wages. Unfair economic pressures and unequal possibilities for women and people who inhabit multiple inter-sectionalities reveal that structural changes are needed because the playing field is uneven. Learning to anger well lets nonbinary people and women stop acquiescing to systems that benefit from their silence. It will take moral grit to instantiate a form of anger as an expression of virtue, and it'll be worth it. Harkening back to the poem poised as a prelude to this book, I would have to say, "This life is very good." So good that it is worth the pain, the fire and spark of anger. Worth figuring out how to do well by one's anger—rooted in the great Loves that animate life, resilient through Sisterhoods of support, courageous enough to call the question, hopeful enough to imagine new futures, and moved to face the source of harm with energy for resistance. There is better living for many people through cultivating agapic anger. Investing in liberation and learning an anger that is self-respecting, loving, hopeful, and courageous is a path toward justice in marginalized communities.

Notes

INTRODUCTION

1 Although there is not a lot of literature yet on nonbinary experiences of anger, I hope this book begins to address this gap, perhaps primarily by exposing it, so that this book lifts people on the beautiful spectrum of gender identities.

2 This project's ethnographic engagement was primarily through participant observation and interviews with four people who are US citizens (Mexican American, Black, white, and Asian American), plus some of their colleagues, from 2018 to 2023. I describe their practices and understandings without a need to generalize them, that is, without implying that the women's actions and words are intended as blanket recommendations for others, regardless of the particular person and context. At the same time, my method brings two other moves alongside description. I introduce theories and think with these theories in light of the organizers' insights, and I invite readers to make their own assessments regarding the ideas and practices that may yield traction in their own lifeworlds. From an intersectional perspective, many voices are not well represented here since all four of the primary interlocutors identify as women with kids.

3 The accounts described here are Mary's, Drea's, Sue's, Kelly's. They do not generalize their stories as if to account for anyone else who is similar to them in some way. I relay their stories and do not suppose or claim generalizability either. I understand their stories as emerging from their locations, wherein they describe their true experience; at the same time, I acknowledge, as I think they would, that some of their stories might be told and understood differently in other local, national, and global contexts where other perspectives may be held.

CHAPTER ONE

1 Esperanza School, http://esperanzacommunity.org/about-us/. "Esperanza Community Services began as a school in 1969, created in response to the lack of services available to students whose learning needs were not being met in traditional classrooms. Our founder, Guadalupe Reyes, was driven to help her son Bobby, whose developmental disabilities were caused by spinal meningitis. Guadalupe Reyes made Esperanza School a place where students with developmental disabilities found a solid foundation of education, support and encouragement upon which they could grow.

Families took notice of our high quality educational services, and Esperanza took root in Chicagoland, building a tradition of working closely with those we serve to provide customized supports that meet the needs of each individual. We added more services to meet the needs of families, including those that help people with developmental disabilities throughout their life. A day program was added to help adults continue to build independent living skills, as was a support program that enabled Esperanza to meet the needs of families in their own homes. A 24-hour residential program was established, allowing adults with developmental disabilities to live with their peers in the community.

For 50 years, Esperanza Community Services has provided support to thousands of students, adult participants and their families. Now, more than ever, Esperanza provides an anchor of support for families across the region. Without our vital programs and services, many of the students and adults that we serve, as well as their families, would have nowhere to turn for support. We developed meaningful relationships that often last well beyond a student's time with us at Esperanza, and we are honored to have served thousands of children and adults with developmental disabilities and their families."

2   El Valor, https://elvalor.org/about/. El Valor means courage. "El Valor was founded in 1973 by the late Guadalupe A. Reyes, a visionary leader and mother who dreamed of a community in which all members—including her son with special needs—could live, learn and work. From its roots in the Hispanic community, El Valor has grown into a nationally recognized multicultural, multipurpose organization with a mission that reaches millions through its International Public Awareness Campaign."

3   From Gamaliel, https://gamaliel.org/about-us/.

4   From Gamaliel, https://gamaliel.org/about-ntosake/.

5   From Gamaliel, https://gamaliel.org/about-ntosake/.

CHAPTER TWO

1   Aristotle, *Rhetoric*, https://tinyurl.com/5yjv33yf; Thomas Aquinas, *Summa Theologiae* (*ST*) (Lander, WY: The Aquinas Institute for the Study of Sacred Doctrine, 2012), I–II 22.3; Jan Schnell and Diana Fritz Cates, "Rethinking Anger as a Desire for Payback: A Modified Thomistic View," *Religions* 10, no. 11 (2019): 14.

2   Ralph Adolphs and David J. Anderson, *The Neuroscience of Emotion: A New Synthesis* (Princeton, NJ: Princeton University Press, 2018), 35.

3   Adolphs and Anderson, *Neuroscience*, 23.

4   Aquinas, *ST*, I-II 46.5.

5   Martin Reuter et al. "The Biological Basis of Anger: Associations with the Gene Coding for DARPP-32 (PPP1R1B) and with Amygdala Volume," *Behavioral Brain Research* 202 (2009): 179.

6   Adolphs and Anderson, *Neuroscience*, 18–19.

7   Adolphs and Anderson, *Neuroscience*, 19.

8   Adolphs and Anderson, *Neuroscience*, 20.

9   Martha C. Nussbaum, *Anger and Forgiveness: Resentment, Generosity, Justice* (New York: Oxford University Press, 2016), 33, 38, 54, 127.

10   Nussbaum, *Anger and Forgiveness*, 24.

11   Schnell and Cates, "Rethinking Anger"; Myisha Cherry, "Anger Is Not a Bad Word," TedxUofIChicago, May 21, 2015, https://www.youtube.com/watch?v=uysTk2EIotw; Macalester Bell, "Anger, Virtue, and Oppression," in *Feminist Ethics and Social and*

Political Philosophy: Theorizing the Non-Ideal, ed. Lisa Tessman (London and New York: Springer, 2009); Lucas A. Swaine, "Blameless, Constructive, and Political Anger," *Journal for the Theory of Social Behavior* 26, no. 3 (1996): 257–74.

12 Schnell and Cates, "Rethinking Anger," 22, 24.

13 See also Aristotle's parallel discussion of *species* of friendship in *Nichomachean Ethics* 8.3, http://classics.mit.edu/Aristotle/nicomachaen.html.

14 Aquinas, *ST*, I-II 46.8.

15 The agapic anger we're describing is already at work in visible publics. A quick review of the news shows Rosa Parks, Nina Simone, Greta Thunberg, Kamala Harris, Elizabeth Warren, and Nancy Pelosi, among others, exhibit the resilience and prosocial actions associated with agapic anger. Peter Dreier, "Rosa Parks: Angry, Not Tired," *Dissent* 53, no. 1 (2006): 88–92; Jeanne Theoharis, "How History Got the Rosa Parks Story Wrong," *The Washington Post*, December 1, 2015, https://www.washingtonpost.com/posteverything/wp/2015/12/01/how-history-got-the-rosa-parks-story-wrong/; Urana McCauley, "Rosa Parks Was My Aunt. It's Time to Set the Record Straight," Shondaland.com, February 4, 2019, https://www.shondaland.com/inspire/a16022001/rosa-parks-was-my-aunt/; Dorian Lynskey, "Nina Simone: 'Are You Ready to Burn Buildings?,'" *The Guardian*, June 22, 2015, https://www.theguardian.com/music/2015/jun/22/nina-simone-documentary-what-happened-miss-simone; Soraya Chemaly, *Rage Becomes Her*; Tom McCarthy, "'Currently Chilling': Greta Thunberg Ridicules Trump's Angry Tweets," *The Guardian*, December 12, 2019, https://www.theguardian.com/us-news/2019/dec/12/trump-angry-tweets-greta-thunberg-prompt-humorous-response-teen-activist; Paul Rincon, "Greta Thunberg: People Underestimate 'Angry Kids,'" *BBC News*, December 3, 2019, https://www.bbc.com/news/science-environment-50644395; Justin Wise, "Greta Thunberg Adds 'Teen Working on Anger Management' to Twitter Bio after Trump Attack," *The Hill*, December 12, 2019, https://thehill.com/homenews/administration/474235-greta-thunberg-adds-teen-working-on-anger-management-problem-to; Avery Blank, "Elizabeth Warren's Anger Propels Campaign: How Outrage Can Help Your Career, Too," *Forbes*, November 12, 2019, https://www.forbes.com/sites/averyblank/2019/11/12/elizabeth-warrens-anger-propels-campaign-how-outrage-can-help-your-career-too/#7e7e32147911; Megan Garber, "The Sexism Is Getting Sneakier: Is Elizabeth Warren Overly 'Angry'? The Media Are Just Asking Questions," *The Atlantic*, November 13, 2019, https://www.theatlantic.com/entertainment/archive/2019/11/elizabeth-warren-and-sneak-sexism/601876/; Gregory Krieg and Eric Bradner, "Elizabeth Warren Responds to 'Angry' Charge: 'I Am Angry and I Own It,'" CNN, November 9, 2019, https://www.cnn.com/2019/11/08/politics/elizabeth-warren-joe-biden-sexism-charges/index.html; Meagan Flynn, "Trump Tried to Insult 'Unhinged' Pelosi with an Image. She Made It Her Twitter Cover Photo," *The Washington Post*, October 17, 2019, https://www.washingtonpost.com/nation/2019/10/17/trump-insults-pelosi-over-meeting-photo-she-made-it-her-twitter-cover/; Amber Phillips, "A Series of Images of Pelosi and Trump Have Made Her a Meme, and for Some, a Symbol of a Woman in Power," *The Washington Post*, October 18, 2019, https://www.washingtonpost.com/politics/2019/10/17/images-pelosi-trump-that-cemented-her-symbol-woman-command/; Poppy Noor, "Trump's Troll-in-Chief? Once Again, Nancy Pelosi Bites Back," *The Guardian*, October 17, 2019, https://www.theguardian.com/us-news/2019/oct/17/nancy-pelosi-trump-meeting-photo-meltdown-battle; Kevin Breuninger, "'Don't Mess with Me'—House Speaker Nancy Pelosi Rips Reporter Who Asks if She Hates Trump," CNBC, December 5,

2019, https://www.cnbc.com/2019/12/05/nancy-pelosi-lashes-out-at-reporter-who-asks-if-she-hates-trump.html.

16 Aquinas, *ST*, I-II 46.4.

17 Schnell and Cates, "Rethinking Anger," 18.

18 Aquinas, *ST*, I-II 47.2.

19 Schnell and Cates, "Rethinking Anger," 18.

20 J. Haidt, "The Moral Emotions," in *Handbook of Affective Sciences*, ed. R. J. Davidson, K. R. Scherer, and H. H. Goldsmith (Oxford: Oxford University Press, 2003), 856.

21 David Kaiser, "How Today's American Crisis Is Different," *Time*, July 22, 2016, https://time.com/4417672/american-crisis-history/; American Public Health Association, "Gun Violence," https://www.apha.org/topics-and-issues/gun-violence; Robinson Meyer, "How Climate Change Could Trigger the Next Global Financial Crisis," *The Atlantic*, August 1, 2019, https://www.theatlantic.com/science/archive/2019/08/how-fed-could-fight-climate-change-adam-tooze/595084/.

22 Martin Luther King Jr., *Why We Can't Wait* (New York: Signet Classic, 2000), 69.

23 Randy Martin, *Critical Moves: Dance Studies in Theory and Politics* (Durham, NC: Duke University Press, 1998), 3.

24 Rebecca Traister, *Good and Mad: The Revolutionary Power of Women's Anger* (New York: Simon & Schuster, 2018), xx.

25 Traister, *Good and Mad*, 243.

26 J. Giles Milhaven, *Good Anger* (New York: Sheed & Ward, 1989), 124.

27 Chemaly, *Rage Becomes Her*, xx.

CHAPTER THREE

1 Hema Georgina Biswas. "Colonialism, Imperialism and White Supremacy," *International Journal of Policy Sciences and Law* 1, no. 1 (September 2020): 414–23.

2 bell hooks, *Killing Rage: Ending Racism* (New York: Henry Holt, 1995), 13.

3 hooks, *Killing Rage*, 14.

4 hooks, *Killing Rage*, 12.

5 Lester Olson, "Anger among Allies: Audre Lorde's 1981 Keynote Admonishing the National Women's Studies Association," *Quarterly Journal of Speech* 97, no. 3 (2011): 288.

6 Sheldene Simola, "Anti-Corporate Anger as a Form of Care-Based Moral Agency," *Journal of Business Ethics* 94 (2010): 266.

7 Cherry "Anger Is Not a Bad Word."

8 Audre Lorde, *Sister Outsider: Essays and Speeches* (Trumansburg, NY: Crossing Press, 1984), 116.

9 Jess Zimmerman, "A Fury's Battle: How Our Culture Demonizes Women's Anger and Protects Abusers," Literary Hub, March 11, 2021, https://lithub.com/a-furys-battle-how-our-culture-demonizes-womens-anger-and-protects-abusers/.

10 Amia Srinivasan, "The Aptness of Anger," *Journal of Political Philosophy* 26, no. 2 (2018): 123–44 (emphasis original).

11 Srinivasan. "The Aptness of Anger," 143.

12 Srinivasan. "The Aptness of Anger," 144.

13   Rachel Simon, "Dear Asian American Girls, Let Yourselves Be Angry," HelloGiggles, March 19, 2021, https://hellogiggles.com/asian-american-girls-anger/. This writing appeared following the deadly March 6, 2021, shooting of six Asian American women in Atlanta.

14   Valerie Kaur, *See No Stranger: A Memoir and Manifesto of Revolutionary Love* (New York: One World, 2020), 126.

15   Valerie Kaur, "Three Lessons of Revolutionary Love in a Time of Rage." TED, November 2017, https://www.ted.com/talks/valarie_kaur_3_lessons_of_revolutionary_love_in_a_time_of_rage?autoplay=true&muted=true&language=en.

16   Brittney Cooper, *Eloquent Rage: A Black Feminist Discovers Her Superpower* (New York: St. Martin's Press, 2018), 2–3. Brittney Cooper capitalizes certain words, e.g., "Angry Black Women" and "Black Women and Girls," throughout her book, a pattern I will follow while discussing her work.

17   E. V. Spelman, in "Anger and Insubordination" (manuscript, 1982), points out that men's cultural permission to be angry bolsters their claim to authority (early version read to midwestern chapter of the Society for Women in Philosophy, spring 1982).

18   Kaur, *See No Stranger*, 117.

19   P. J. Quartana and J. W. Burns, "Painful Consequences of Anger Suppression," *Emotion* 7, no. 2 (2007): 400–14, https://doi.org/10.1037/1528-3542.7.2.400.

20   Chemaly, *Rage Becomes Her*, 25.

21   S. Helen Chukka, communication to author, January 1, 2024.

22   Cooper, *Eloquent Rage*, 274.

23   Myisha Cherry, "On James Baldwin and Black Rage," *Critical Philosophy of Race* 10, no. 1 (2022): 16.

24   Seneca, *De Ira*, https://en.wikisource.org/wiki/Of_Anger/Book_I, 3.

25   Unless otherwise noted, biblical quotes are from the NRSV.

26   See, for example, Robert E. Sinkewicz's chapter "On the Eight Thoughts," in *Evagrius of Pontus: The Greek Ascetic Corpus* (Oxford: Oxford University Press, 2003), 66–90.

27   Luther's Works Tischreden 1:311, no. 660.

28   Selina Rachel Stone. "Holy Spirit, Holy Bodies? Pentecostal Spirituality, Pneumatology, and the Politics of Embodiment" (master's thesis, The University of Birmingham, 2021), 208.

29   Kira Austin-Young, "What Should We Do with Angry Women?," *Ministry Matters*, September 25, 2018, https://www.ministrymatters.com/all/entry/9277/what-should-we-do-with-angry-women.

30   Nathan DeSalvo, "How Gender Shapes Anger and Aggression" (master's thesis, Rhode Island College, 2023), https://digitalcommons.ric.edu/cgi/viewcontent.cgi?article=1437&context=etd.

31   DeSalvo, "How Gender Shapes Anger and Aggression," 31.

32   Hilary Malatino, "Tough Breaks: Trans Rage and the Cultivation of Resilience," *Hypatia* 34, no. 1 (2019): 121–40, at 121.

33   Ephrem Fernandez and Kathleen Malley-Morrison, "Gender-Inclusive and Gender-Informed Treatment of Anger," in *Treatments for Anger in Specific Populations: Theory, Application, and Outcome*, ed. Ephrem Fernandez (New York: Oxford Academic, 2015), 213–35.

34 M. Budziszewska and K. Hansen, "'Anger Detracts from Beauty': Gender Differences in Adolescents' Narratives about Anger," *Journal of Adolescent Research* 35, no. 5 (2020): 635–64.

35 N. Legate, R. M. Ryan, and N. Weinstein. "Is Coming Out Always a 'Good Thing'? Exploring the Relations of Autonomy Support, Outness, and Wellness for Lesbian, Gay, and Bisexual Individuals," *Social Psychological and Personality Science* 3 (2012): 16.

36 Brooke N. Petersen, *Religious Trauma: Queer Stories in Estrangement and Return* (Lanham, MD: Lexington Books/Fortress Academic, 2022), 5.

37 Petersen, *Religious Trauma*, 18. Here Petersen is calling on the work of L. S. Brown, "Sexuality, Lies, and Loss: Lesbian, Gay, and Bisexual Perspectives on Trauma," *Journal of Trauma Practice* 2 (2003): 38.

38 Jen McWeeny. "Liberating Anger, Embodying Knowledge: A Comparative Study of María Lugones and Zen Master Hakuin," *Hypatia* 25, no. 2 (Spring 2010): 295–315, at 295.

39 Traister, *Good and Mad*.

40 Soraya Chemaly, "The Power of Women's Anger," Ted Talks, February 28, 2019. https://www.youtube.com/watch?v=wMt0K-AbpCU.

41 Agneta H. Fischer and Catharine Evers, "Anger in the Context of Gender," in *International Handbook of Anger: Constituent and Concomitant Biological, Psychological, and Social Processes,* ed. Michael Potegal, Gerhard Stemmler, and Charles Spielberger (New York: Sprinter New York, 2010), 349–60.

42 Soraya Chemaly, "Soraya Chemaly on the Power of Women's Rage," SOH Talks and Ideas Archive, March 17, 2019, https://www.youtube.com/watch?v=e5C9VqjqfGY.

43 Miriam Greenspan, "Feminism, Therapy, and Changing the World," *Women & Therapy* 40, no. 3/4 (2017): 340.

CHAPTER FOUR

1 McNair Scholars is an award for undergraduates showing strong academic potential designed to prepare them for advanced "studies through involvement in research and other scholarly activities," https://mcnairscholars.com/about/.

2 Chicago Coalition for the Homeless, https://www.chicagohomeless.org/.

3 MYSI, "President's Message" May 22, 2023, https://www.myschicago.org/about/presidents-message/.

CHAPTER FIVE

1 Jean Porter, *Moral Action and Christian Ethics* (Cambridge: Cambridge University Press, 1999), 181.

2 Aquinas, *ST*, II-II 58.12.

3 Paul Woodruff, "Anger: Justice in the Soul," in *The Ajax Dilemma: Justice, Fairness, and Rewards* (New York: Oxford University Press, 2011), 163.

4 The emotion of despair also has a relationship to hope, but it implies a loss of hope in some previous goal alongside a movement to withdraw (Aquinas, *ST*, I-II 40.1, 40.4).

Despair and sadness are emotions that can occur when hope is lost, often surfacing when unjust injury occurs.

5 Aquinas, *ST*, II-II 123.2.

6 Aquinas, *ST*, I-II 45.2.

7 Aquinas, *ST*, II-II 123.10 *ad* 3.

8 Aquinas, *ST*, II-II 123.10 *ad* 3.

9 Saul Alinsky, *Reveille for Radicals* (New York and Toronto: Random House, 1969), ix.

10 Diana Fritz Cates, Religious Ethics: Religion and Emotion, class taught at the University of Iowa, Iowa City, Iowa, January 28, 2019.

11 Diana Fritz Cates, "Toward an Ethic of Shared Selfhood," *The Annual of the Society of Christian Ethics* 11 (1991): 250.

12 Cates, "Toward an Ethic of Shared Selfhood," 252.

13 Aristotle, *Nichomachean Ethics* 1156b6–11.

14 Patrick Lee Miller, "Finding Oneself with Friends," in *The Cambridge Companion to Aristotle's "Nichomachean Ethics,"* ed. Ronald Polansky (Cambridge: Cambridge University Press, 2014), 246.

15 Aristotle, *Nichomachean Ethics* 1172a10.

16 Charles Duhigg, "The Real Roots of American Rage," *The Atlantic*, January/February 2019, https://www.theatlantic.com/magazine/toc/2019/01/.

17 University of Texas, "Ethics: Overconfidence Bias," https://ethicsunwrapped.utexas.edu/glossary/overconfidence-bias.

18 Scribbr, Overconfidence Bias, https://www.scribbr.com/research-bias/overconfidence-bias/.

19 Schnell and Cates, "Rethinking Anger," 24.

20 Schnell and Cates, "Rethinking Anger."

CHAPTER SIX

1 Susan Leigh Foster, "Choreography," In Terms of Performance (website), http://intermsofperformance.site/keywords/choreography/susan-leigh-foster.

2 Susan Leigh Foster, "The Ballerina's Phallic Pointe," in *Corporealities: Dancing Knowledge, Culture, and Power*, ed. Susan Leigh Foster (New York, London: Routledge, 1996), 7.

3 Susan Leigh Foster, "Choreographies of Protest," *Theatre Journal* 55 (2003): 395.

4 Foster, "Protest," 397.

5 Foster, "Protest," 412. "The process of creating political interference calls forth a perceptive and responsive physicality that, everywhere along the way, deciphers the social and then choreographs an imagined alternative. As people fathom injustice, organize to protest, craft a tactics [sic], and engage in action, their bodies read what is happening and articulate their imaginative rebuttal."

6 Rebekah J. Kowal, *How to Do Things with Dance: Performing Change in Postwar America* (Middletown, CT: Wesleyan University Press, 2010), 1.

7 Kowal, *How to Do Things with Dance*, 5.

8 Kowal, *How to Do Things with Dance*, 255. "Activists took the potential of action to a new level in its application for the transformation of everyday life. Using similar tools

and techniques as those being pioneered in postwar modern dance, they formulated new approaches to attaining social justice and cultivated mental and physical capacities to exert their oppositional consciousness."

9 Kowal, *How To Do Things with Dance*, 235.

10 "Unprincipled absence" refers both to Aristotle's understanding that it is blameworthy to fail to have anger in instances of legitimate slight, and the organizers' sense that it is problematic to not permit injustices to stir up one's anger and/or to avoid giving credence to one's anger.

11 Aquinas, *ST*, 46.1, 46.2.

12 Woodruff, "Anger," 167.

CHAPTER EIGHT

1 Aristotle, *Nichomachean Ethics* 1103b1–1103b3.

2 "Continue to Learn and Grow," Prime Focus Goalkeeping (website), https://www.primefocusgoalkeeping.com/single-post/2018/11/13/continue-to-learn-and-growa-look-inside-the-mind-of-world-cup-veteran-alyssa-naeher.

3 Aquinas, *ST*, I-II 56.5.

4 Diana Fritz Cates, *Aquinas on the Emotions: A Religious-ethical Inquiry* (Washington, DC: Georgetown University Press, 2009), 3.

5 Aristotle, *Nichomachean Ethics* 2.6.

6 Seneca, *De Ira*, 3.

7 Seneca, *De Ira*, 1.

8 Aristotle, *Rhetoric*.

9 Aristotle, *Nicomachean Ethics* 1125b.

10 Aquinas, *ST*, I-II 12–17.

11 Aquinas, *ST*, I-II 55.3.

12 Cates, personal communication, September 3, 2019.

13 Aquinas, *ST*, I-II 18.

14 Aquinas, *ST*, I-II 18. I have enumerated the four criteria in the opposite order from Aquinas's list. Aquinas also names one basic commitment that remains true regardless of the presence or absence of the other criteria: a thing or action attains a measure of goodness whenever it does what it is meant to do. Take dynamite for example: when dynamite explodes, it has done what it is to do, and there is a measure of goodness in that. Consider the action of talking: when a person talks and communication occurs, there is a measure of goodness in that.

15 Aquinas, *ST*, I-II 18.4.

16 How is it that place of context differs from circumstance? I take a circumstance to include facts, events, etc. that make a situation the way it is—a set of conditions. I take place (or in this case the context of relationships) to be an aspect that could be considered a part of the circumstance of an action.

17 Evangelical Lutheran Church in America, "A Social Message on Immigration," elca.org, 1998, https://tinyurl.com/bdbjrt7j.

18 United States Conference of Catholic Bishops, "Catholic Social Teaching on Immigration and the Movement of Peoples," usccb.org, http://www.usccb.org/issues-and-action/human-life-and-dignity/immigration/

catholic-teaching-on-immigration-and-the-movement-of-peoples.cfm. Their statement cites the same passages from Leviticus and Matthew as found in the statement from Sue's faith community.

19 United States Conference of Catholic Bishops, "Catholic Social Teaching."

20 United States Conference of Catholic Bishops, "Catholic Social Teaching."

21 The United Methodist Church: Church & Society, "Immigration to the US," umcjustice.com, https://www.umcjustice.org/what-we-care-about/civil-and-human-rights/immigration-to-the-united-states.

22 United Methodist Church: Church & Society, "Immigration to the US."

23 Drea's non-denominational church does not have similar data posted.

24 Aristotle, *Nichomachean Ethics* 1125b.

25 Michael T. Koch and Sarah A. Fulton, "In the Defense of Women: Gender, Office Holding, and National Security Policy in Established Democracies," *The Journal of Politics* 73, no. 1 (2011): 4.

26 Mariela V. Campuzano, "Force and Inertia: A Systematic Review of Women's Leadership in Male-dominated Organizational Cultures in the United States," *Human Resource Development Review* 18, no. 4 (2019): 439.

27 Aquinas, *ST*, I-II 48.3.

CHAPTER NINE

1 Aristotle, *Rhetoric*.

2 Aquinas, *ST*, I-II 46.7.

3 Aquinas, *ST*, I-II 47.1.

4 Aquinas, *ST*, I-II 47.1. Throughout the *Summa Theologica*, Aquinas cites intellectual adversaries, apparently responding to actual debates of his time.

5 Aquinas, *ST*, I-II 47.1 (italics added).

6 Aquinas, *ST*, I-II 47.1. I slightly amended this translation to better reflect that the original Latin used a noun, *vindictam*.

7 Aquinas, *ST*, I-II 47.1.

8 Aquinas, *ST*, I-II 47.2.

9 Hyaeweol Choi's *Gender and Mission Encounters in Korea: New Women, Old Ways* (Berkeley: University of California Press, 2009) explores women's compliance and resistance in religious publics, showing that women often simultaneously comply with and resist certain ideas and practices as they negotiate their ways of being in community. Her insights shed light on patterns of resistance and compliance expressed by the organizers as they navigate patriarchally embedded behaviors exhibited by loving (grand)fathers.

10 Cherry, "Anger Is Not a Bad Word."

11 For more on cultural appropriation see Maisha Z. Johnson's "What's Wrong with Cultural Appropriation? These 9 Answers Reveal Its Harm," The Good Men Project, December 3, 2019, https://goodmenproject.com/featured-content/whats-wrong-with-cultural-appropriation-these-9-answers-reveal-its-harm/. See also my article "Resisting Cultural Appropriation in Hymnody," *CrossAccent* 29, no. 3 (2021).

12 Aquinas, *ST*, I-II 47.2.

13 Aquinas, *ST*, I-II 47.3.

14 This line of inquiry was inspired by Diana Cates's public lecture at the University of Iowa, "The Morality of Payback: A Critique of Aquinas's Account of Anger," April 9, 2019.

15 Michael P. Jaycox, "The Black Lives Matter Movement: Justice and Health Equity," *Health Progress* 43, no. 6 (2016): 42–47.

16 Aquinas, *ST*, I-II 48.2.

17 Matthijs Baas, Carsten K. W. De Dreu, and Bernard A. Nijstad, "Creative Production by Angry People Peaks Early on, Decreases over Time, and Is Relatively Unstructured," *Journal of Experimental Social Psychology* 47, no. 6 (2011): 1109.

18 Aquinas, *ST*, I-II 48.2.

19 Lisa Tessman, *Burdened Virtues: Virtue Ethics for Liberatory Struggles* (New York: Oxford University Press, 2005), 106.

20 Tessman, *Burdened Virtues*, 106.

21 Seneca, *De Ira*.

22 Aquinas, *ST*, I-II 29.1.

23 Aquinas, *ST*, I-II 46.3 *ad* 2.

24 Aquinas, *ST*, II-II 34.3.

25 Aquinas, *ST*, I-II 29.2 *ad* 2.

26 Aquinas, *ST*, I-II 96.4.

27 Aquinas, *ST*, I-II 97.2.

28 Aquinas, *ST*, II-II 34.5 *ad* 3.

CHAPTER TEN

1 Alaska and New York have boroughs, while Louisiana has parishes and other states have counties.

2 No equivalent English translation exists.

3 Victoria Hutter, "Bearing the Unbearable: The Art of Gaman," National Endowment for the Arts, 2010, https://www.arts.gov/art-works/2010/bearing-unbearable-art-gaman. See also "The Art of Gaman," National Parks Conservation Association, Fall 2011, https://www.npca.org/articles/1001-the-art-of-gaman.

4 *Nisei* refers to the first generation of children born in the United States to Japanese American immigrants. The immigrating parents (*Iisei*) are first generation, and *Nisei* are second generation. *Sansei* are the children of Nisei—so *Sansei* are third generation. *Yonsei* are the children of *Sansei*; therefore, they are considered the fourth generation from an immigration standpoint.

CHAPTER ELEVEN

1 Susan L. Engh, *Women's Work: The Transformational Power of Faith-Based Community Organizing* (Lanham, MD: Lexington Books/Fortress Academic, 2019), 27.

2 Engh, *Women's Work*, 29.

3 Engh, *Women's Work*, 3.

4 Engh, *Women's Work*, 3.

5 Engh, *Women's Work*, 3.

6 While organizers attempt for respondents to be free to answer as is true for them, I also recognize that the organizer usually inhabits a position of power within the room and many factors, including cultural conditioning, make people feel more or less free to disagree with authority figures or people they want to impress.

7 Aquinas, *ST*, I-II 18.2.

8 A more extensive power analysis would be beneficial to assess the ways in which the youth's resistance dance was capable of righting wrongs.

9 Audre Lorde, "The Uses of Anger," *Women's Studies Quarterly* 9, no. 3 (1981): 7–10.

10 Engh, *Women's Work*, 106.

11 Valerie Kaur, quoted in "The Three Practices of Revolutionary Love," Justice Conversation (website), https://justiceconversation.org/2019/02/11/the-three-practices-of-revolutionary-love/.

12 This does not mean that anger toward an individual is unimportant; the need to deal with one-to-one anger in a one-to-one manner is just not the focus of this book.

13 Aquinas, *ST*, I-II 18.4.

14 Engh, *Women's Work*, 134.

15 Martin Luther King Jr., "Honoring Dr. DuBois," speech delivered at Carnegie Hall, New York City, February 23, 1968, https://www.ushistory.org/documents/dubois.htm.

16 Engh, *Women's Work*, 37.

17 Engh, *Women's Work*, 39.

18 Tali Hatuka, *The Design of Protest: Choreographing Political Demonstrations in Public Space* (Austin: University of Texas Press, 2018), 266.

CHAPTER TWELVE

1 Joann Ellison Rodgers, "Go Forth and Anger," *Psychology Today*, March 11, 2014, https://www.psychologytoday.com/us/articles/201403/go-forth-in-anger.

2 Rodgers, "Go Forth and Anger."

3 Myisha Cherry, "Anger, Motivation, and Productivity," working paper, University of Illinois Chicago, 2014.

4 Judith Barad, "Aquinas and the Role of Anger in Social Reform," *Logos: A Journal of Catholic Thought and Culture* 3, no. 1 (2000): 132.

5 Myisha Cherry, "Myisha Cherry Talks Race, Anger, and Social Change at University of New England," YouTube, June 6, 2016, https://www.youtube.com/watch?v=li7EF-YrVD4.

6 Engh, *Women's Work*, 109.

7 Engh, *Women's Work*, 109–10.

8 For example, Mary said, "You become less of a victim if people come to understand that you've got this in your pocket and you're very willing to use it."

9 Mary connected anger's role in helping people understand identity to this story: "What kind of a female is this who figured out how to escape that?!' And not only escape it but build a powerful and exciting life of her own. So, it begins to define who she is—you are the kind of woman who survives and thrives!"

10 Chemaly, "The Power of Women's Anger."

References

Abu-Lughod, Lila. *Writing Women's Worlds: Bedouin Stories.* Berkeley: University of California Press, 2008.

Adolphs, Ralph, and David J. Anderson. *The Neuroscience of Emotion: A New Synthesis.* Princeton, NJ: Princeton University Press, 2018.

Ahmed, Sara. "Affective Economies." *Social Text* 22, no. 2 (79) (2004): 117–39.

Albers, Robert H. *Ministry with Persons with Mental Illness and Their Families.* Minneapolis: Fortress Press, 2012.

Alinsky, Saul. *Reveille for Radicals.* New York and Toronto: Random House, 1969.

American Psychological Association. *Diagnostic and Statistical Manual of Mental Disorders.* 5th ed. Washington, DC: American Psychiatric Press, 2013.

———. "How to Recognize and Deal with Anger." apa.org, March 2, 2022. https://www.apa.org/helpcenter/recognize-anger.

American Public Health Association. "Gun Violence." apha.org. https://www.apha.org/topics-and-issues/gun-violence.

Anthropology@Princeton. "What Is Ethnography?" Princeton University. Accessed July 25, 2024. https://anthropology.princeton.edu/programs/ethnographic-studies/what-ethnography.

Aquinas, Saint Thomas. *Summa Theologiae.* Translated by Laurence Shapcote. Edited by John Mortensen and Enrique Alarcón. Lander, WY: The Aquinas Institute for the Study of Sacred Doctrine, 2012.

Aristotle. *Nichomachean Ethics.* Accessed July 25, 2024. http://classics.mit.edu/Aristotle/nicomachaen.html.

———. *Rhetoric.* Accessed July 25, 2024. https://tinyurl.com/5yjv33yf.

Austin-Young, Kira. "What Should We Do with Angry Women?" *Ministry Matters*, September 25, 2018. https://www.ministrymatters.com/all/entry/9277/what-should-we-do-with-angry-women.

Baas, Matthijs, Carsten K. W. De Dreu, and Bernard A. Nijstad. "Creative Production by Angry People Peaks Early on, Decreases over Time, and Is Relatively Unstructured." *Journal of Experimental Social Psychology* 47, no. 6 (November 2011): 1107–15.

Banet-Weiser, Sarah. "Empowered: Media, Gender, and the Economies of Visibility." McGranahan Lecture, University of Iowa, April 19, 2018.

———. *Empowered: Popular Feminism and Popular Misogyny*. Durham, NC: Duke University Press Books, 2018.

Barad, Judith. "Aquinas and the Role of Anger in Social Reform." *Logos: A Journal of Catholic Thought and Culture* 3, no. 1 (2000): 124–44.

Bell, Macalester. "Anger, Virtue, and Oppression." In *Feminist Ethics and Social and Political Philosophy: Theorizing the Non-Ideal*, edited by Lisa Tessman, 165–83. London and New York: Springer, 2009.

Berberich, Christine, Neil Campbell, and Robert Hudson. "Affective Landscapes: An Introduction." *Cultural Politics* 9, no. 3 (November 2013): 313–22. https://doi.org/10.1215/17432197-2347000.

Berlant, Lauren. *Cruel Optimism*. Durham, NC: Duke University Press, 2011.

———. "Lauren Berlant Interview." IPAK.Centar, November 28, 2016. https://www.youtube.com/watch?v=Ih4rkMSjmjs.

Blank, Avery. "Elizabeth Warren's Anger Propels Campaign: How Outrage Can Help Your Career, Too." *Forbes*, November 12, 2019. https://www.forbes.com/sites/averyblank/2019/11/12/elizabeth-warrens-anger-propels-campaign-how-outrage-can-help-your-career-too/#7e7e32147911.

Blanton, Thomas, IV, and Raymond Pickett, eds. *Paul and Economics: A Handbook*. Minneapolis: Fortress Press, 2017.

Blunt, Alison, and Gillian Rose, eds. *Writing Women and Space: Colonial and Postcolonial Geographies*. New York: Gulliford Press, 1994.

Breuninger, Kevin. "'Don't Mess with Me'—House Speaker Nancy Pelosi Rips Reporter Who Asks If She Hates Trump." CNBC, December 5, 2019. https://www.cnbc.com/2019/12/05/nancy-pelosi-lashes-out-at-reporter-who-asks-if-she-hates-trump.html.

Budziszewska, M., and K. Hansen. "'Anger Detracts from Beauty': Gender Differences in Adolescents' Narratives about Anger." *Journal of Adolescent Research* 35, no. 5 (2020): 635–64. https://journals.sagepub.com/doi/10.1177/0743558419845870.

Cairns, Douglas. "Emotions." In *The Encyclopedia of Ancient History*, edited by Roger S. Bagnall et al. Hoboken, NJ: John Wiley & Sons, 2017. https://doi.org/10.1002/9781444338386.wbeah30086.

Campuzano, Mariela V. "Force and Inertia: A Systematic Review of Women's Leadership in Male-Dominated Organizational Cultures in the United States." *Human Resource Development Review* 18, no. 4 (2019): 437–69.

Carver, Charles S., and Eddie Harmon-Jones. "Anger Is an Approach-Related Affect: Evidence and Implications." *Psychological Bulletin* 135, no. 2 (2009): 183–204. https://doi.org/10.1037/a0013965.

Cates, Diana Fritz. "Approaching the Morality of Emotion: Specifying the Object of Inquiry." In *Feeling Emotion*, edited by John Corrigan, 23–52. Durham, NC, and London: Duke University Press, 2017.

———. *Aquinas on the Emotions: A Religious-Ethical Inquiry.* Washington, DC: Georgetown University Press, 2009.

———. *Choosing to Feel: Virtue, Friendship, and Compassion for Friends.* South Bend: University of Notre Dame Press, 1997.

———. Personal communication. August 29, 2019.

———. Personal communication. September 3, 2019.

———. Personal communication. January 24, 2020.

———. "Relational Complexity and Ethical Responsibility." *Journal of Religious Ethics* 47, no. 1 (2019): 154–65.

———. Religious Ethics: Religion and Emotion. Class taught at the University of Iowa, Iowa City, Iowa, Spring 2019.

———. "Taking Women's Experience Seriously: Thomas Aquinas and Audre Lorde on Anger." In *Aquinas and Empowerment: Classical Ethics for Ordinary Lives*, edited by G. Simon Harak, SJ, 47–88. Washington, DC: Georgetown University Press, 1996.

———. "Toward an Ethic of Shared Selfhood." *The Annual of the Society of Christian Ethics* 11 (1991): 249–57.

Center for Disease Control and Prevention. "Coronavirus Disease 2019 (COVID-19): Cases in the US." Last accessed April 28, 2020. https://www. cdc.gov/coronavirus/2019-ncov/cases-updates/cases-in-us.html.

Chemaly, Soraya. "Anger Is Fire for Creativity—and It's Time to Let It Burn." Ideas.Ted.Com, September 11, 2018. https://ideas.ted.com/anger-is-fire-for-creativity-and-its-time-to-let-it-burn/.

———. "The Power of Women's Anger." Ted Talks, February 28, 2019. https://www.youtube.com/watch?v=wMt0K-AbpCU.

———. *Rage Becomes Her: The Power of Women's Anger.* New York: Atria Books, 2018.

———. "Soraya Chemaly on the Power of Women's Rage." SOH Talks and Ideas Archive, March 17, 2019. https://www.youtube.com/watch?v=e5C9VqjqfGY.

Cherry, Myisha. "Anger Is Not a Bad Word." TedxUofIChicago, May 21, 2015. https://www.youtube.com/watch?v=uysTk2EIotw.

———. "Anger, Motivation, and Productivity." Working Paper, University of Illinois, Chicago, 2014.

———. "On James Baldwin and Black Rage." *Critical Philosophy of Race* 10, no. 1 (2022): 16.

———. "Myisha Cherry Talks Race, Anger, and Social Change at University of New England." YouTube, June 9, 2016. https://www.youtube.com/watch?v=li7EF-YrVD4.

Choi, Hyaeweol. *Gender and Mission Encounters in Korea: New Women, Old Ways.* Berkeley: University of California Press, 2009.

Cooper, Brittney. *Eloquent Rage: A Black Feminist Discovers Her Superpower.* New York: St. Martin's Press, 2018.

Copeland, Jordan. "Rehearsals for Engagement: The Moral, Practice of Friendship and the Cultivation of Social Concern." PhD dissertation, University of Iowa, 2007.

de Certeau, Michel. 1984. *The Practice of Everyday Life.* Translated by Steven F. Rendall. Berkeley, Los Angeles, and London: University of California Press, 1984.

Deleuze, Gilles. "On Spinoza." Lectures by Gilles Deleuze, 1978. http://deleuzelectures.blogspot.com/2007/02/on-spinoza.html.

DeSalvo, Nathan. "How Gender Shapes Anger and Aggression." Master's thesis, Rhode Island College, 2023.

Dilley, Paul. Genealogies of Religion. Class taught at the University of Iowa, Iowa City, Iowa, Spring 2019.

Dreier, Peter. "Rosa Parks: Angry, Not Tired." *Dissent* 53, no. 1 (2006): 88–92.

Duhigg, Charles. "The Real Roots of American Rage." *The Atlantic*, January/February 2019. https://www.theatlantic.com/magazine/archive/2019/01/charles-duhigg-american-anger/576424/.

El Valor. "About El Valor." Last accessed June 18, 2024. https://elvalor.org/about/.

Engh, Susan L. *Women's Work: The Transformational Power of Faith-Based Community Organizing.* Lanham, MD: Lexington Books/Fortress Academic, 2019.

Online Etymology Dictionary. "Vengeance." Last accessed June 18, 2024. https://www.etymonline.com/word/vengeance.

Evangelical Lutheran Church in America. "A Social Message on Immigration." ELCA.org, 1998. https://tinyurl.com/bdbjrt7j.

Fernandez, Ephrem, and Kathleen Malley-Morrison. "Gender-Inclusive and Gender-Informed Treatment of Anger." In *Treatments for Anger in Specific Populations: Theory, Application, and Outcome*, edited by Ephrem Fernandez, 213–35. New York: Oxford Academic, 2015.

Finch, Martha L. *Dissenting Bodies: Corporealities in Early New England.* New York: Columbia University Press, 2010.

Fischer, Agneta H., and Catharine Evers. "Anger in the Context of Gender." In *International Handbook of Anger: Constituent and Concomitant Biological, Psychological, and Social Processes*, edited by Michael Potegal, Gerhard Stemmler, and Charles Spielberger, 349–60. New York: Springer New York, 2010.

Flynn, Meagan. "Trump Tried to Insult 'Unhinged' Pelosi with an Image. She Made It Her Twitter Cover Photo." *The Washington Post*, October 17, 2019. https://www.washingtonpost.com/nation/2019/10/17/trump-insults-pelosi-over-meeting-photo-she-made-it-her-twitter-cover/.

Ford, Brett Q., and Maya Tamir. "When Getting Angry Is Smart: Emotional Preferences and Emotional Intelligence." *Emotion* 12, no. 4 (2012): 685–89.

Foster, Susan Leigh. "The Ballerina's Phallic Pointe." In *Corporealities: Dancing Knowledge, Culture, and Power*, edited by Susan Leigh Foster, 1–24. New York and London: Routledge, 1996.

———. "Choreographies of Gender." *Signs: Journal of Women in Culture and Society* 24, no. 1 (1998): 1–33.

———. "Choreographies of Protest." *Theatre Journal* 55 (2003): 395–412.

———. *Choreographing Empathy: Kinesthesia in Performance.* New York and London: Routledge, 2011.

———. "Choreography." In Terms of Performance (website). Accessed June 18, 2024. http://intermsofperformance.site/keywords/choreography/susan-leigh-foster.

———. *Choreography and Narrative: Ballet's Staging of Story and Desire.* Bloomington: Indiana University Press, 1996.

Gade, Anna. *Perfection Makes Practice: Learning, Emotion, and the Recited Quran in Indonesia.* Honolulu: University of Hawai'i Press, 2004.

Gamaliel. n.d. "Ntosake." Accessed June 18, 2024. https://gamaliel.org/our-work/ntosake/.

Garber, Megan. "The Sexism Is Getting Sneakier: Is Elizabeth Warren Overly 'Angry'? The Media Are Just Asking Questions." *The Atlantic*, November 13, 2019. https://www.theatlantic.com/entertainment/archive/2019/11/elizabeth-warren-and-sneak-sexism/601876/.

Goldie, Peter, ed. *The Oxford Handbook of Philosophy of Emotion.* New York: Oxford University Press, 2010.

Gonzalez, Justo L. *The Story Luke Tells: Luke's Unique Witness to the Gospel.* Grand Rapids, MI: William B. Eerdmans, 2015.

Greenspan, Miriam. "Feminism, Therapy, and Changing the World." *Women & Therapy* 40, no. 3/4 (2017): 334–45.

Griffin, Rachel Alicia. "I AM an Angry Black Woman: Black Feminist Autoethnography, Voice, and Resistance." *Women's Studies in Communication* 35, no. 2 (2012): 138–57.

Grossberg, Lawrence. *We Gotta Get Out of This Place: Popular Conservatism and Postmodern Culture.* New York and London: Routledge, 1992.

Haidt, J. "The Moral Emotions." In *Handbook of Affective Sciences,* edited by R. J. Davidson, K. R. Scherer, and H. H. Goldsmith, 852–70. Oxford: Oxford University Press, 2003.

Hatuka, Tali. *The Design of Protest: Choreographing Political Demonstrations in Public Space.* Austin: University of Texas Press, 2018.

Helion, C., and D. A. Pizarro. "Beyond Dual-Processes: The Interplay of Reason and Emotion in Moral Judgment." In *Handbook of Neuroethics* edited by J. Clausen and N. Levy, 109–25. Dordrecht: Springer, 2015.

hooks, bell. *Killing Rage: Ending Racism.* New York: Henry Holt, 1995.

Infed. "Donald Schon (Schön): Learning, Reflection, and Change." Accessed June 18, 2024. https://infed.org/mobi/donald-schon-learning-reflection-change/.

Jaycox, Michael P. "The Black Lives Matter Movement: Justice and Health Equity." *Health Progress* 97, no. 6 (2016): 42–47.

———. "The Civic Virtues of Social Anger: A Critically Reconstructed Normative Ethic for Public Life." *Journal of the Society of Christian Ethics* 36, no. 1 (2016): 123–43.

Johnson, Maisha Z. "What's Wrong with Cultural Appropriation? These 9 Answers Reveal Its Harm." The Good Men Project, December 3, 2019. https://goodmenproject.com/featured-content/whats-wrong-with-cultural-appropriation-these-9-answers-reveal-its-harm/.

Kaiser, David. "How Today's American Crisis Is Different." *Time,* July 22, 2016. https://time.com/4417672/american-crisis-history/.

Kaur, Valerie. *See No Stranger: A Memoir and Manifestor of Revolutionary Love.* New York: One World, 2020.

———. "Three Lessons of Revolutionary Love in a Time of Rage." TED, November 2017. https://www.ted.com/talks/

valarie_kaur_3_lessons_of_revolutionary_love_in_a_time_of_rage?aut oplay=true&muted=true&language=en

Keys, Mary M. *Aquinas, Aristotle, and the Promise of the Common Good.* Cambridge and New York: Cambridge University Press, 2006.

King, Martin Luther, Jr. "Honoring Dr. DuBois." Speech delivered at Carnegie Hall, New York City, February 23, 1968. https://www.ushistory.org/documents/dubois.htm.

———. *Why We Can't Wait.* With an afterword from the Reverend Jesse L. Jackson Sr. New York: Signet Classic, 2000.

Koch, Michael T., and Sarah A. Fulton. "In the Defense of Women: Gender, Office Holding, and National Security Policy in Established Democracies." *The Journal of Politics* 73, no. 1 (2011): 1–16.

Kowal, Rebekah J. *How to Do Things with Dance: Performing Change in Postwar America.* Middletown, CT: Wesleyan University Press, 2010.

Kowal, Rebekah J., and Gerald Siegmund. *The Oxford Handbook of Dance and Politics.* New York: Oxford University Press, 2017.

Krieg, Gregory, and Eric Bradner. "Elizabeth Warren Responds to 'Angry' Charge: 'I Am Angry and I Own It.'" CNN, November 9, 2019. https://www.cnn.com/2019/11/08/politics/elizabeth-warren-joe-biden-sexism-charges/index.html.

Laclau, Ernesto. "Why Do Empty Signifiers Matter to Politics?" In *Post-Marxism, Populism and Critique,* 66–74. London and New York: Routledge, 2005.

LaMothe, Kimerer L. *Between Dancing and Writing: The Practice of Religious Studies.* New York: Fordham University Press, 2004.

———. *Why We Dance: A Philosophy of Bodily Becoming.* New York: Columbia University Press, 2015.

Legate, N., R. M. Ryan, and N. Weinstein. "Is Coming Out Always a 'Good Thing'? Exploring the Relations of Autonomy Support, Outness, and Wellness for Lesbian, Gay, and Bisexual Individuals." *Social Psychological and Personality Science* 3 (2012): 145–52.

Lévi-Strauss, Claude. *Introduction to the Work of Marcel Mauss.* London: Routledge, 1987.

Logos. "Bible Word Study." Accessed June 18, 2024. https://tinyurl.com/2mz5u6xa.

Lorde, Audre. *Sister Outsider: Essays and Speeches.* Trumansburg, NY: Crossing Press, 1984.

———. "The Uses of Anger." *Women's Studies Quarterly* 9, no. 3 (1981): 7–10.

Lundy, Colleen. *Social Work and Social Justice: A Structural Approach to Practice*. Peterborough, ON: Broadview Press, 2004.

Lynskey, Dorian. "Nina Simone: 'Are You Ready to Burn Buildings?'" *The Guardian*, June 22, 2015. https://www.theguardian.com/music/2015/jun/22/nina-simone-documentary-what-happened-miss-simone.

Maggi, Wynne. *Our Women Are Free: Gender and Ethnicity in the Hindukush*. Ann Arbor: University of Michigan Press, 2001.

Malatino, Hilary. "Tough Breaks: Trans Rage and the Cultivation of Resilience." *Hypatia* 34, no. 1 (2019): 121–40.

Martin, Randy. *Critical Moves: Dance Studies in Theory and Politics*. Durham, NC: Duke University Press, 1998.

———. "Overreading 'The Promised Land': Towards a Narrative of Context in Dance." In *Corporealities: Dancing Knowledge, Culture, and Power*, edited by Susan Leigh Foster, 177–98. New York and London: Routledge, 1996.

Matsuda, Mari J. 1991. "Beside My Sister, Facing the Enemy: Legal Theory Out of Coalition." *Stanford Law Review* 43, no. 6 (1991): 1183–92.

McCarthy, Tom. "'Currently Chilling': Greta Thunberg Ridicules Trump's Angry Tweets." *The Guardian*, December 12, 2019. https://www.theguardian.com/us-news/2019/dec/12/trump-angry-tweets-greta-thunberg-prompt-humorous-response-teen-activist.

McCauley, Urana. "Rosa Parks Was My Aunt. It's Time to Set the Record Straight." Shondaland.com, February 4, 2019. Transcribed by Liz Dwyer. https://www.shondaland.com/inspire/a16022001/rosa-parks-was-my-aunt/.

Meyer, Robinson. "How Climate Change Could Trigger the Next Global Financial Crisis." *The Atlantic*, August 1, 2019. https://www.theatlantic.com/science/archive/2019/08/how-fed-could-fight-climate-change-adam-tooze/595084/.

Milhaven, Giles. *Good Anger*. New York: Sheed & Ward, 1989.

Miller, Patrick Lee. "Finding Oneself with Friends." In *The Cambridge Companion to Aristotle's "Nicomachean Ethics,"* edited by Ronald Polansky, 319–49. Cambridge: Cambridge University Press, 2014.

Noor, Poppy. "Trump's Troll-in-Chief? Once Again, Nancy Pelosi Bites Back." *The Guardian*, October 17, 2019. https://www.theguardian.com/us-news/2019/oct/17/nancy-pelosi-trump-meeting-photo-meltdown-battle.

Nussbaum, Martha C. *Anger and Forgiveness: Resentment, Generosity, Justice.* New York: Oxford University Press, 2016.

Olson, Lester C. "Anger among Allies: Audre Lorde's 1981 Keynote Admonishing the National Women's Studies Association." *Quarterly Journal of Speech* 97, no. 3 (2011): 283–308.

Petersen, Brooke N. *Religious Trauma: Queer Stories in Estrangement and Return.* Lanham, MD: Lexington Books/Fortress Academic, 2022.

Phillips, Amber. "A Series of Images of Pelosi and Trump Have Made Her a Meme, and for Some, a Symbol of a Woman in Power." *The Washington Post,* October 18, 2019. https://www.washingtonpost.com/politics/2019/10/17/images-pelosi-trump-that-cemented-her-symbol-woman-command/.

Pickett, Raymond. *The Cross in Corinth: The Social Significance of the Death of Jesus.* London: Sheffield Academic Press, 1997.

Pickett, Ray. Personal communication. Lutheran School of Theology at Chicago, 2015.

Pope, Stephen J., ed. *The Ethics of Aquinas.* Washington, DC: Georgetown University Press, 2002.

Porter, Jean. "Dispositions of the Will." *Philosophia* 41 (2013): 289–300. https://doi.org/10.1007/s11406-013-9430-9.

———. *Justice as a Virtue: A Thomistic Perspective.* Grand Rapids, MI: Eerdmans, 2016.

———. *Moral Action and Christian Ethics.* Cambridge: Cambridge University Press, 1999.

———. *The Recovery of Virtue: The Relevance of Aquinas for Christian Ethics.* Louisville, KY: John Knox Press, 1990.

Quartana, P. J., and J. W. Burns. "Painful Consequences of Anger Suppression." *Emotion* 7, no. 2 (2007): 400–14.

Rawls, John. *A Theory of Justice.* Cambridge, MA: Harvard University Press, 1971.

Reeder, John P., Jr. "What Kind of Person Could Be a Torturer?" *Journal of Religious Ethics* 38, no. 1 (2010): 67–92.

Reuter, Martin, Bernd Weber, Christian J. Fiebach, Christian Elger, and Christian Montag. "The Biological Basis of Anger: Associations with the Gene Coding for DARPP-32 (PPP1R1B) and with Amygdala Volume." *Behavioral Brain Research* 202 (2009): 179–83.

Ricoeur, Paul. "Hermeneutics of Testimony." In *Essays on Biblical Interpretation,* 119–54. Philadelphia: Fortress Press, 1980.

Rincon, Paul. 2019. "Greta Thunberg: People Underestimate 'Angry Kids.'" *BBC News*, December 3, 2019. https://www.bbc.com/news/science-environment-50644395.

Rodgers, Joann Ellison. "Go Forth and Anger." *Psychology Today*, March 11, 2014. https://www.psychologytoday.com/us/articles/201403/go-forth-in-anger.

Roseman, Ira J. 2018. "Functions of Anger in the Emotion System." In *The Function of Emotions: When and Why Emotions Help Us*, edited by Heather C. Lench, 141–73. New York: Springer, 141–73.

Schaefer, Donovan O. *Religious Affects: Animality, Evolution, and Power.* Durham, NC: Duke University Press, 2015.

Schnell, Jan Rippentrop. "Resisting Cultural Appropriation in Hymnody." *CrossAccent* 29, no. 3 (2021): 8–25.

Schnell, Jan Rippentrop, and Diana Cates. "Rethinking Anger as a Desire for Payback: A Modified Thomistic View." *Religions* 10, no. 11 (2019): 618–49. https://doi.org/10.3390/rel10110618.

Schön, Donald A. *The Reflective Practitioner: How Professionals Think in Action.* New York: Basic Books, 1983.

Seneca. *De Ira.* Wikisource. Accessed June 18, 2024. https://en.wikisource.org/wiki/Of_Anger/Book_I.

Simola, Sheldene K. "Anti-Corporate Anger as a Form of Care-Based Moral Agency." *Journal of Business Ethics* 94 (2010): 255–69.

Sinkewicz, Robert E. "On the Eight Thoughts." In *Evagrius of Pontus: The Greek Ascetic Corpus*, 66–90. Oxford: Oxford University Press, 2003.

Snow, Nancy E. "Introduction." In *The Oxford Handbook of Virtue*, edited by Nancy E. Snow, 1–6. Oxford: Oxford University Press, 2018.

Srinivasan, Amia. "The Aptness of Anger." *Journal of Political Philosophy* 26, no. 2 (2018): 123–44.

Stacy, Kelli. 2019. "US Goalkeeper Alyssa Naeher, a Connecticut Native, Inspires Home State with Recent Success." *Hartford Courant*, July 10, 2019. https://www.courant.com/sports/hc-sp-alyssa-naeher-uswnt-connecticut-native-20190706-20190611-mx5ukkph6vfk5p5nycyhj6gbmy-story.html.

Stichter, Matthew. "The Skill of Virtue." PhD dissertation, Bowling Green State University, 2007. https://tinyurl.com/548kca33.

Stone, Selina Rachel. "Holy Spirit, Holy Bodies? Pentecostal Spirituality, Pneumatology, and the Politics of Embodiment." Master's thesis, The University of Birmingham, 2021.

Stout, Jeffrey. "Commitments and Traditions in the Study of Religious Ethics." *Journal of Religious Ethics* 25, no. 3 (1998): 23–56.

Supp-Montgomerie, Jenna. "Affect and the Study of Religion." *Religion Compass* 9/10 (2015): 335–45.

Swaine, Lucas A. "Blameless, Constructive, and Political Anger." *Journal for the Theory of Social Behavior* 26, no. 3 (1996): 257–74.

Taves, Ann. *Religious Experience Reconsidered: A Building-Block Approach to the Study of Religion and Other Special Things*. Princeton, NJ: Princeton University Press, 2011.

Tessman, Lisa. *Burdened Virtues: Virtue Ethics for Liberatory Struggles*. New York: Oxford University Press, 2005.

Theoharis, Jeanne. 2015. "How History Got the Rosa Parks Story Wrong." *The Washington Post*, December 1, 2015. https://www.washington-post.com/posteverything/wp/2015/12/01/how-history-got-the-rosa-parks-story-wrong/.

Thurman, Howard. *Jesus and the Disinherited*. New York: Abingdon-Cokesbury Press, 1949.

Traister, Rebecca. *Good and Mad: The Revolutionary Power of Women's Anger*. New York: Simon & Schuster, 2018.

———. Rebeccatraister.com. Accessed June 18, 2024. http://www.rebecca-traister.com.

United Methodist Church: Church & Society. "Immigration to the US." umcjustice.org. Accessed June 18, 2024. https://www.umcjustice.org/what-we-care-about/civil-and-human-rights/immigration-to-the-united-states.

United States Conference of Catholic Bishops. "Catholic Social Teaching on Immigration and the Movement of Peoples." usccb.org. Accessed June 18, 2024. http://www.usccb.org/issues-and-action/human-life-and-dignity/immigration/catholic-teaching-on-immigration-and-the-movement-of-peoples.cfm.

West, Cornel. "Justice Is What Love Looks Like in Public." Sermon delivered at Howard University, 2011. https://www.youtube.com/watch?v=nGqP7S_WO6o&feature=youtu.be&t=21s.

Westberg, Daniel. *Right Practical Reason: Aristotle, Action, and Prudence in Aquinas*. Oxford: Clarendon Press, 1984.

Wise, Justin. "Greta Thunberg Adds 'Teen Working on Anger Management' to Twitter Bio after Trump Attack." *The Hill*, December 12, 2019. https://

thehill.com/homenews/administration/474235-greta-thunberg-adds-teen-working-on-anger-management-problem-to.

Wood, W. Jay. "Christian Theories of Virtue." In *The Oxford Handbook of Virtue*, edited by Nancy E. Snow, 281–300. Oxford: Oxford University Press, 2018.

Woodruff, Paul. "Anger: Justice in the Soul." In *The Ajax Dilemma: Justice, Fairness, and Rewards*, 162–69. New York: Oxford University Press, 2011.

Zimmerman, Jess. "A Fury's Battle: How Our Culture Demonizes Women's Anger and Protects Abusers," Literary Hub, March 11, 2021. https://lithub.com/a-furys-battle-how-our-culture-demonizes-womens-anger-and-protects-abusers/.